What You Need to Know About: Terror

Micah Halpern

WHAT YOU NEED TO KNOW ABOUT: TERROR

The Toby Press

The Toby Press
First Edition 2003

The Toby Press LLC
POB 8531, New Milford, CT. 06676-8531, USA
& POB 2455, London WIA 5WY, England
www.tobypress.com

ISBN 1 59264 026 5, *paperback*

A CIP catalogue record for this title is
available from the British Library

Typeset in Garamond by Jerusalem Typesetting

Printed and bound in the United States by
Thomson-Shore Inc., Michigan

*I dedicate this book to everyone
who has been touched by terror*

*To the innocent who were murdered
To the innocent who were injured*

*To lives that have been changed forever
To lives that have been destroyed*

To heroes and to heroines

Why are despots like Saddam Hussein, Kim Il Jung, and Robert Mugabe so effective? How do terrorists like Osama bin Laden bring the free world to its knees? What can be done to protect ourselves from the likes of these men and others?

These questions have preoccupied me for years. Now, with each passing day, especially after 9/11, they are all the more significant.

A few answers to questions that preoccupy us all—some of us ask them every day, some of us dare not ask them aloud.

Micah Halpern, 2003

Contents

Terror: Q&A

Major Terrorist Organizations

Resources

Introduction

Terror is not new. It's just that until recently Americans didn't see it as a significant issue.

Terrorists in Beirut targeted US peacekeepers in 1983, killing 307 and wounding 241. New York's World Trade Center was bombed in 1993, killing 6 and wounding 1,000. Terrorists in Saudi Arabia targeted US citizens in 1996, killing 19. There were simultaneous bombings against US embassies in Kenya and Tanzania in 1998, in which 263 people were killed and 5,000 injured (mostly locals). The US naval ship USS Cole was attacked in 2000, killing 17. These events never made an impact.

Not until September 11, 2001. That's when it all changed—for the terrorists and for us, the objects of their terror.

For those who sponsor and support terror, for those who quietly and not so quietly applaud terrorist actions and activities, 9/11 was a proud day. On that day the world took notice. For years, terrorists had tried to slay the evil infidel, and on 9/11 they succeeded. They had received a sign from above that the unbeliever was not invincible, that terror would triumph.

That's what they think. But they are wrong.

It is precisely *because* terrorists were so very successful on that fateful, horrific day that they will now fail. The simultaneous hijacking of four planes resulting in the deaths of more than 3,000 people, in devastation that we cannot yet fathom, is exactly why—from here on—terror is doomed to fail. Today America knows that terror is a real and serious threat; probably the single *greatest* threat to freedom and democracy.

Once upon a time, terror was motivated by politics. The terror of today has its roots in psychological intimidation and is based almost exclusively on religious extremism and Islamic fundamentalism.

Historically, terror developed out of more conventional ways of waging war and oppressing subject peoples. Conquerors of old used threats of terrible pain as a tool to flaunt strength and demand compliance—which, in most cases, involved the promise not to revolt, the payment of taxes, and lip service allegiance to the ruler. After each military victory, a Roman Legion would instill fear and trepidation in the populations it conquered by destroying monuments and symbols important to the vanquished enemy, and leaving their ruins standing. Future generations saw the vanquished relics as evidence of the power and might of Rome. When the Romans destroyed the Temple in Jerusalem in 70 AD, they also hung and crucified Jerusalemites and left them to rot on trees and stakes outside the city. They wanted to intimidate everyone who arrived in Jerusalem, to show them what happens to a society that attempts to revolt against mighty Rome. Carthage was another case in point. The center of power of the Phoenicians, it was finally conquered by Rome in 146 BC, after a series of three wars. Rome was so advanced in the techniques of destruction that ships full of salt were sent to poison the ground of Carthage so that it could never again threaten Roman world hegemony.

Many governments or tribes persecuted particular segments of the population they ruled over even within times of peace, often because their beliefs differed from those of the ruling elite. In 1060 AD, an elite group of highly motivated people in the Levant surrounded a charismatic Muslim leader named Hassan ben Sabbah and were given a mission—to convince all others of the rightness of ben Sabbah's particular interpretation of Islam. Those who were reluctant to change their ways were targeted and murdered. Hassan ben Sabbah was systematically perpetrating assassinations against people for what they believed—or, in this case, for what they did not believe. If it were an entire group that refused to comply with his teachings, ben Sabbah would order a hit against the leader of the group or clan.

This elite group was called assassins, from the Arabic word *hashashin* (in plural); eaters or chewers of hashish. They struck fear into the hearts of other Muslim leaders and their followers. The assassins were also known as *fedayeen*—men who would sacrifice their lives—a term still used today by several terrorist organizations, and the name chosen by Saddam Hussein for his elite, private corps of soldiers. The assassins also applied their talents to assassinating Crusaders. Ben Sabbah's *fedayeen* dwindled in strength after his death.

Modern terror as we understand it began in the 18ᵗʰ century. The name itself comes from the term "reign of terror" which was coined to refer to the period of the French Revolution from 1793–1794, when French revolutionary leader Maximilien Marie Isidore Robespierre and his Committee of Public Safety arrested over 200,000 people and beheaded many thousands simply because they were connected to the aristocracy, or for 'treasonable activity'—which included any counter-revolutionary activity. In this way, Robespierre consolidated his own regime by killing his enemies and intimidating the potential opposition. Robespierre's favorite method for beheading was the guillotine. Conservative estimates put the number of people he beheaded at 12,000—liberal estimates would nearly double that.

In 1866, after the Civil War in the United States, the Ku Klux Klan was formed in order to intimidate all those who supported the ideas of reconstruction, unification, and freedom for slaves. They performed acts of terror, including intimidation and the destruction of property, and even lynching.

It wasn't until the latter half of the 19ᵗʰ century that terror moved into its next stage, with attacks aimed at governments and policy makers. The anarchist movement believed that all forms of government were oppressive and should be abolished, and they were committed to overthrowing established governments using non-peaceful means. Assassinations and bombings became their primary tools. These terrorists, who made use of the threat of assassination as well as actual assassinations, frightened and intimidated leaders and countries around the world. A Russian anarchist assassinated Czar Alexander II in 1881. In the United States, fears of an anarchist revolution grew. Chicago's Haymarket Square was bombed in 1886 by an anarchist.

Alexander Berkman assassinated steel magnate Henry Frick in 1892. Leon Czolgosz assassinated President William McKinley in 1901. Both Berkman and Czolgosz were avowed anarchists. A law was passed preventing anarchists from entering the United States.

Ultimately, the anarchist revolution never occurred, and US democracy was stable and attractive enough to enable redress of grievances through its political system. The anarchists and their followers fell in with the general communist movement sweeping through the world.

That, however, did not mean the end of terror. What it did mean was a new trend in terrorist tactics, actions and goals. Anarchists were replaced by Marxist-Leninists-Maoists, and the most politically extreme of all, Muslim fundamentalists—and the brunt of their wrath fell on the United States of America. As reported in a 1997 Pentagon report, fully *one-third* of all terrorist attacks in the 20th century have been against American targets.

A Puerto Rican nationalist terrorist organization, the FALN, attempted to assassinate US President Harry S. Truman in 1950. Five years later they sprayed the US Congress with bullets, wounding five Congressmen.

In 1956, the French were targeted by the Algerian independence terrorist group, the FLN, whose aim was to make the price of French colonialism in Algeria unbearable. Forty-nine Frenchmen living in Algeria were murdered over a three-day period as a response to France's execution of two FLN leaders.

US Attorney-General Robert F. Kennedy was assassinated by Sirhan Sirhan, a Palestinian immigrant to the United States, on June 5, 1968.

The Munich Olympics of 1972 were marred by a terrorist attack in which 11 Israeli athletes were massacred by Palestinian terrorists, members of the PLO.

The most prominent, extreme, terrorist organizations in this group, but certainly not the only ones wielding terror as a tool for change, are those of the Islamic fundamentalists. These are the terrorist organizations most bent on destroying the United States.

Islamic fundamentalists see the United States as their enemy.

and refer to it as the 'big Satan.' In their quest for a world run according to strict Islamic tradition, the military and economic power of the United States is anathema. They see the United States as a land of infidels, the modern heir of Christendom, which has been their traditional enemy throughout hundreds of years of warfare. The great success of non-Muslim states is totally contrary to the political and psychological self-perceptions of Islam. If the United States is the 'big Satan,' Israel is the 'little Satan,' and it too must be destroyed.

1983 was one of the most devastating years of terror perpetrated by Islamic fundamentalists in US history. On April 8, *Hezbollah*, a Lebanese terrorist group sponsored by Iran, bombed the US embassy in Beirut. Seventeen Americans were killed. On October 23 a suicide truck bomb rocked the city of Beirut. It destroyed the US Marine barracks, killing 290 marines asleep in their beds and wounding another 241. The suicide truck bomb had also been planted by the *Hezbollah*, the 'Party of God.' They were attacking Americans because they believed that the United States was siding with the Christian Lebanese against the Muslim Lebanese in their civil war.

In December 1988, two Libyan intelligence agents bombed Pan Am Flight 103, causing it to explode over Lockerbie, Scotland. Of the 270 people murdered, 200 were Americans, many of them college students on their way home for Christmas.

In mainland America, on February 26, 1993, seven-and-a-half years before 9/11, *al Qaeda* attacked the World Trade Center for the first time. Six people were killed and one thousand wounded when a car bomb that the terrorists had planted in the underground parking lot of the Twin Towers exploded. Ramzi Yossef, the leader of the cell that carried out the attack, was arrested in Pakistan in 1995. His arrest foiled an attempt to simultaneously hijack twelve US airliners and blow them up over the Atlantic. At Yossef's trial, he described *al Qaeda's* objectives in the World Trade Center attack. They had hoped to create a domino effect that would bring both buildings down, resulting in 250,000 deaths. He also described how his terrorist group assassinated Israeli Knesset member Rabbi Meir Kahane in May of 1990.

Nineteen US airmen were murdered in Dhahran, Saudi Arabia,

on June 25, 1996. A truck bomb was placed outside the Khobar Towers where they were quartered.

Throughout all these tragedies, tears were shed as people mourned their loved ones, but not one policy was changed. Unfortunately, these acts of terror—attempted assassinations and successful assassinations, truck bombs, exploding planes, the murder of innocent men, women and children, civilians and soldiers—weren't enough to make the United States comprehend the depth of the terrorist menace. People were not yet able to understand the enormity of the threat that was about to invade and change their lives and outlooks forever.

And then, on September 11, 2001, the Twin Towers fell and the Pentagon went up in flames. The reality of terror and of hatred could no longer be ignored or explained away. Since then, the real war against terror has begun. The United States has taken on the responsibility of obliterating terror from this world. It won't be completed in our lifetimes, but it will happen. Terror is evil. Freedom will triumph.

Terror: Q&A

TERROR DEFINED

Question 1:
What is Terror?

ANSWER: Terror is the use of violence or the threat of violence against people or governments to achieve a particular goal or agenda.

ANALYSIS: The motto of the terrorist is "injure one and frighten tens of thousands, kill one and frighten millions."

The goal of the terrorist is single-minded. By arbitrarily and unpredictably attacking civilian targets, terrorists want to strike fear into the hearts of every citizen and force them to change their lives. They achieve their aim by frustrating daily life and normalcy, and disrupting society. If you are too scared to go to the bank, or the movie theatre, or a restaurant, or to get on a train or bus because you fear for your life, then the society around you will rapidly degenerate. Ultimately, terrorists hope that this will create an unstable society in which leaders and policy makers will give in to their demands out of fear for the safety of their citizens.

It makes no difference what the political agenda or ultimate goal of the terrorist group is, the modus operandi, the techniques they use, are always the same. Strike with fear, cause injury and death, and paralyze the public that does not comply with your demands.

Question 2:
Are there different types of terror?

ANSWER: Yes, terror comes in various forms. The simplest model is to divide terror into two categories: religious terror and political terror.

ANALYSIS: The difference between religious terror and political terror is motivation. Even with differing motivation, both types of terrorist groups often join forces to attack a common target.

The religious terrorist believes that he, she, or their organization is fulfilling God's will by murdering heretics. The goal of this terrorist is to rid the world of infidels, of unbelievers and sinners. In their worldview, unbelievers are seen as a threat to their religious philosophy and practice. This terrorist is unsympathetic to anyone who is different and who does not believe what he believes. In the 1998 edict Osama bin Laden published when he founded his organization 'The International Islamic Front for *Jihad* Against the Jews and Crusaders', he stated "We—with God's help—call on every Muslim who believes in God and wishes to be rewarded to comply with God's order to kill the Americans and plunder their money wherever and whenever they find it."

Religious terrorists can be found in nearly every religion. Muslim extremists attack American and Jewish targets around the world. Six Israelis were arrested in 2002 for attempting to blow up a Muslim school on the Mount of Olives. All six were linked to the outlawed organizations Kach and Kahane Chai, which had been banned as racist by the Israeli Supreme Court several years earlier. Christian anti-abortionists bomb abortion clinics and attack doctors who perform abortions.

Political terrorists terrorize and murder civilians in order to change the status quo, to influence a vote, or change a policy. Society is held hostage so that the terrorists may fight the perceived injustice and to draw attention to their political cause. Political terrorists run the gamut from the extreme right—fascists and national extremists such as neo-Nazi groups—to the extreme left—anarchists and communists such as the Japanese Red Army and the Red Brigades of Italy.

Terrorists are always extremists, whether religious or political—that's what motivates their terror.

Question 3:
What does a terrorist look like?

ANSWER: Terrorists look just like everyone else. That is what makes finding them so difficult.

ANALYSIS: One of the greatest strengths of democracy is also the source of its vulnerability: its freedoms and its openness to different people from different backgrounds make democracy a very easy target for terrorists.

A terrorist should be defined by actions, not by external appearance or background. That being said, there are certain countries, such as Iran and Libya, that are avowed enemies of the West and the citizens of those countries, when they enter the free world, should be scrutinized and investigated. That's where profiling comes in (see also Question 59).

There have been instances of female terrorists masquerading as pregnant women, knowing that Western men will be less likely to scrutinize and search them. In April 2002, a female suicide bomber disguised as a pregnant woman blew herself up in an open-air market in Jerusalem. In the late 1950s, the Algerian terrorist group FLN gave bombs to attractive young women who would sit in cafés and wait for French soldiers to approach them—at which point they would blow themselves up. A female suicide bomber assassinated Rajiv Gandhi, and nearly a third of all suicide attacks in Sri Lanka have been carried out by women.

Once terrorists have infiltrated into a Western democracy it is nearly impossible to find them or identify them until after they have carried out an attack. Even then, some still manage to hide or escape. The only good way to find terrorists is through informants and through shared intelligence with other nations and agencies.

Question 4:
How and why do terrorists select targets?

ANSWER: Targets are selected for three reasons: symbolic value, maximum impact, and ease of access and execution.

ANALYSIS: The terrorist will choose a target because it symbolizes an aspect of the enemy, and is the antithesis of the terrorist organization's priorities and values. The World Trade Center symbolizes the economic success of America, and the Pentagon its military might—which is why they were perfect targets for *al Qaeda*, an organization that has declared *jihad* (holy war) on America.

As well as their symbolic value, the World Trade Center and the Pentagon also fulfilled another requirement—an attack at these sites achieved maximum impact because the densely populated buildings provided a huge number of casualties.

Accessibility is the other factor a terrorist will consider. How easy or difficult it is to get in and out without detection will affect the success of the attack.

From the point of view of a terrorist, if a target fulfills all three requirements it is ideal—but even if only one or two factors are present, the site is still at risk for targeting. A suicide bomber will only worry about getting *to* a target, not about getting away.

Question 5:
Are there different definitions as to what constitutes an act of terror?

ANSWER: Yes, and they can be very confusing.

ANALYSIS: The FBI stipulates that for an attack to be called an act of terror, a recognized terrorist group or organization must carry it out. That definition does not take into account the possibility of an individual not affiliated with a terrorist group perpetrating an act of terror. The FBI calls those hate crimes. Other law enforcement agencies and countries around the world define terror by the objectives of the perpetrator(s) and the identity of the target(s). The Department of Defense classifies any attack against an Army base or a marine barracks as terror. In Britain, the police and MI5 view any attack against a British institution as a terror attack.

Due to these differing definitions of what constitutes terror, there are often confusing, mixed messages after an attack, as to whether or not what took place was actually an act of terror.

From the simple point of view of 'spin' the FBI and other agencies have an interest in labeling these attacks as individual hate crimes rather than elevating them to the level of terrorist attacks. It is easier to calm the nerves of a nation or a community after a hate crime than after an act of terror. On July 4, 2002, in LAX airport in Los Angeles, Hesham Mohamed Hadayat, an Egyptian living in America, shot and killed two people at the EL AL check-in counter. The FBI officially termed it a hate crime. Almost a year later, in April 2003, after a thorough investigation was completed and long after the publicity around the incident had died down, they changed their classification of the incident to an act of terror.

There is an inconsistency in definition and a double standard at play.

Question 6:

Due to the differences in defining terror, are there different approaches to the issue of how to deal with a captured terrorist?

ANSWER: Yes. And those differences can be the cause of terrible tragedy.

ANALYSIS: The biggest problem with the difference in approach to terror is the issue of terrorist's rights. In the case of ordinary criminals caught in the midst of committing a crime, once subdued they are disarmed and arrested, after which follows an investigation and then a trial. That cannot be the case with terrorists. A terrorist, even when seemingly subdued, might still be armed or booby-trapped with a bomb. The ideal situation for terrorists is to wait for the moment when people surround them—particularly if they are law enforcement officers—and detonate. With a simple movement, the press of a button, many people will die. Mission accomplished.

The standard anti-terrorist procedure is to create a safe area by moving a terrorist away from populated areas, sometimes even through using a robot. The terrorist's clothes are then stripped away to determine that there is, indeed, no bomb on the body. Then comes the arrest. However, sometimes it is impossible to move the live, subdued, disabled, potential terrorist's body to a safe place. What you have to do, if that is the case, is to kill the terrorist. Even though it sounds cold-blooded, even though law enforcement authorities have an overwhelming need to interrogate the terrorist, there is no alternative. To act otherwise would be to endanger the lives of innocent bystanders. The chance of others being killed is too great and outweighs the issues of due process.

A prime example of this preventative measure occurred

during the attack discussed in the previous question, at LAX airport in California on July 4, 2002. When Hesham Mohamed Hadayat opened fire, killing two people, an Israeli security officer at the scene subdued him, and then, to the horror of the American public, killed him. Shocking as it seemed, it was a post 9/11 lesson in anti-terrorist disarmament and survival. The US criminal justice system is not quite set up for this situation because it hasn't yet confronted this kind of terror—for a while there was concern that the security officer would be charged.

Question 7:
Can there be good terror and bad terror?

ANSWER: No, there is no good terror. It is just an excuse to justify mass murder.

ANALYSIS: Calling any deed an act of terror labels it for most of the world as beyond the pale. It immediately establishes the perpetrators as unworthy of attention or legitimacy. Due to this, many terrorist groups attempt to whitewash or justify their actions. Certain leaders contribute to this whitewashing by emphasizing a distinction between acts of violence and acts of terror. By calling an attack an act of violence rather than an act of terror, they are lessening the impact of the attack, and lending it a form of legitimacy.

In an interview with failed suicide bombers in Israel, one terrorist was asked what crimes children have committed that they deserve to be targeted. He answered "Those children are Jews and when they grow up what will they become? They will become soldiers..." Palestinian terrorists also assert that any Israeli attacked in the disputed territories of the West Bank and Gaza are legitimate targets simply because they are there, in that particular place. To them, even blowing up a pizza parlor in Jerusalem is justifiable, and therefore an act of violence, or 'good terror' because it is a valid target and fair game.

Unfortunately, even Western officials succumb to this twisted logic.

Murdering civilians is always terror, wherever they are. Yet while the United States regularly sends representatives to pay condolence calls on family members of Americans killed in terrorist attacks in Israel, it does not always send representatives if the victim lived in the West Bank or Gaza. Creating categories of 'legitimate targets' is a dangerous precedent. After all, in a video transcript, Osama bin

Laden stated: "Our terrorism is a good accepted terrorism because it's against America"—clearly an unacceptable definition of legitimacy.

Similarly, many leaders lend legitimacy to terrorists by sympathizing with their grievances. While they condemn an act of terror such as 9/11, they contend that the terrorists who attacked the Twin Towers had an important point concerning America. "The United States brought this upon itself," they say. "The terror, the 'understandable violence', was a result of flawed perceptions and bad foreign policy," they say. In an article in *Business Week*, French Green party member Noël Mamère was quoted as saying "the reality is that American policy could only result in the kind of terrorism we've just seen."

Wrong. Whether or not grievances are legitimate, they never justify terror. The more one tries to create distinctions the more ridiculous the definitions become. The murder of innocents is just that—murder.

Question 8:
Is it terror when terrorists attack soldiers?

ANSWER: That depends on whom you ask. Some say that terror can only be perpetrated against innocent civilians.

ANALYSIS: This is a question that is debated by all: the military, the press, policy makers, pundits and scholars. Each views the world through their own individual prism and arrives at a different definition for non-war acts of violence against the military.

Everyone agrees that terror is a violent act or series of acts perpetrated knowingly against innocent civilians outside the laws of war. Everyone agrees that the 9/11 attacks were acts of terror—they were perpetrated against civilians. However, is it terrorism when the same terrorist organization (*al Qaeda*) blows up a US naval ship, as it did the USS Cole, in October 2000, in Yemen? The United States said "yes," that was an act of terror.

However, is it terror when the *Hamas* terrorist organization attacks an Israeli army post or vehicle? The United States and other world governments say "no." They also change their definitions of terror when Palestinian *Tanzim* (civilian militia) enter West Bank settlements (over Israel's green line which demarcates land acquired only after the 1967 War) and murder children. Most governments say that isn't terror, even though the victims are civilians. Yet, when those same *Tanzim* attack Israelis within the green line, the world says "yes, that's terror."

The messages and the definitions are very confusing and con-tradictory. What the State Department says about Israel and the West Bank and what the Department of Defense says about its American soldiers are two different things.

Whichever definition of terror you assume to be correct, the tragedy and great loss of human life remain unchanged. This disparity between definitions, the individual assessment of each act after it has been perpetrated, brings with it a new definition—terror as defined by politics, not policy.

Question 9:
Why do people disagree as to whether terror has occurred?

ANSWER: Different agendas. Different definitions.

ANALYSIS: As the saying goes, "one man's terrorist is another man's freedom fighter." There will always be justification of terrorist attacks by supporters of terror and these supporters will always try to whitewash acts of terror by choosing euphemisms to describe the attacks. Those reactions aside, there are other reasons why people see the same thing and refer to it differently.

Victims of attacks are much quicker to label the experience as terror than are officials. Law enforcement officials are wary of using the 'terror' word unless they are absolutely, positively, 100% sure that it is terror and cannot be anything else. Before law enforcement agencies label an attack as terror they must be certain of the motive, the organization, and the identity of the perpetrator(s).

The time lag this creates and the different terms used by various agencies and eye witnesses can often lead to confusion, false reporting and even worse—total misunderstanding of the threat.

As we have already discussed, in most cases the FBI is reluctant to refer to anything as terror, and when they do, it must almost always be organized and connected to a group. By their standard definition, an individual acting on their own cannot and will not be defined as a terrorist except in very unusual circumstances. And that designation comes long after the public fanfare is over. The reclassification of the LAX airport attack came almost a year after the attack.

In November 1990, outside the New York Hilton Hotel, Rabbi Meir Kahane, the leader of an extremist Jewish group, was assassinated by El-Sayid Nasir, an Egyptian Islamist who was a member of *al Qaeda* and was linked to the 1993 World Trade Center bombing plot.

El-Sayid Nasir was convicted on "weapons charges" in connection with Kahane's killing. Far from being convicted of a terrorist act, he wasn't even convicted of murder.

Question 10:

Isn't terror a legitimate political response? Terrorists often claim they are fighting injustice in the only way they can. How else are people supposed to get their point across?

ANSWER: Terror is not politics. The murder of civilians can never be justified no matter what the motivation.

ANALYSIS: Many people are familiar with the argument that terror is the only tool available to people who do not have an army to fight their wars for them. They see them as guerrilla warriors, freedom fighters, using the only tool they have to fight a larger, more powerful, and better-equipped enemy. They assert that if the playing field were level they would fight using the rules of war.

Leaving aside the fact that many religious terrorists publicly proclaim their goal as the destruction of all infidels, and a level playing field would simply give them more ammunition to commit mass murder, this is a dangerously simplistic and misleading argument. The inhumanity of the terrorist method in and of itself invalidates the claims of a terrorist group. It is a contradiction in terms to profess your aims as the achievement of freedoms and human rights for one group of people through the indiscriminate terrorizing and murder of another group. Targeting civilian populations is murder, and one does not play politics with murderers. As Benjamin Netanyahu, former Prime Minister of Israel, said, "Those who deliberately bomb babies are not interested in freedom, and those who trample on human rights are not interested in defending such rights." In World War II, with France overrun by the Nazis, the French Resistance worked to destroy the Nazi occupation, but they did not consider attacking German women and children, that would have been an act of terrorism, not war.

Those who are genuinely interested in finding a just resolution to their cause can use methods other than terror to accomplish their aims. Resistance through non-violent means, including civil disobedience, peaceful demonstrations, boycotts, lobbying, and petitioning are all options. Peaceful change is possible.

Question 11:
Why is it important to fight terror?

ANSWER: If Western democracies do not attack the roots of terror, then control of the free world will be held captive to the whims of any extremist movement or individual with a bomb or a gun.

ANALYSIS: Terror has existed for decades, but Western democracies had believed that a certain degree of terror was inevitable and therefore tolerable. 9/11 changed that, and a policy of zero tolerance for terrorism has been instituted. The United States has gone in search of terrorists and their global networks.

In order to fight terror you must pull it out by the roots. The supporters and funders of terror and those people who give terrorists sanctuary are all now being targeted by the United States and its allies. Charities and foundations that fund terrorist organizations are being identified and closed down—over one hundred million dollars in assets belonging to terrorist organizations have been frozen, in 145 countries around the world. The invasions of Afghanistan and Iraq were carried out in order to curb terrorist regimes.

Question 12:
How long will the fight against terror take?

ANSWER: Due to the conscious effort now being made, we have a strong chance to win the battle against terror—but the fight will take decades.

ANALYSIS: Sadly, it took 9/11 to awaken the Western world to the dangers of terror and to the realization that it cannot be ignored, and must be fought. It is not an easy battle. Exact identifications of terrorists must be made and that is not easily done. Terrorist organizations, their members, supporters, and bases—every element must be searched out.

Fighting terror takes significant energy and serious money. It will take an entirely new approach and mindset to solve the problem of security. Most importantly, it will take a revamping of intelligence agencies, and new methods of evaluating and analyzing information, and cooperation between information-gathering forces.

What once seemed insignificant, or too impossible to happen, has to be reckoned with. The danger lies in becoming too jumpy; the fight against terror must go on, but normal, everyday life must continue as well.

Conclusions

- Creating fear through violence does not make the terrorist right.
- Do not accept word games when people try to make any distinction between types of terror. Terror is terror. It is never a legitimate response to a political situation. Do not allow any person, country, or organization to convince you otherwise.
- Never give in to terrorist demands or surrender to their tactics.
- Attack terror at the source; the best defense is a good offense. Do not wait for terrorists to strike before searching them out.
- Use intelligence gathering apparatus to destroy infrastructures and confiscate money sources. Use legal and military means to eradicate terrorist organizations.
- Expose those who protect, sponsor, and quietly condone terror. There is no distinction between those who raise money for terrorist goals and the terrorists who murder.
- Be vigilant and observant, but do not be afraid. Be aware and cautious of people who look or act differently, but do not let fear of terrorism alter your lifestyle.
- Good security at high-risk sites is not only necessary and important, it is a crucial deterrent. The harder it is to carry out a successful attack, the less likely it is for that site to be chosen.
- Prepare for the long haul. Terrorism will not simply stop, and therefore the West cannot stop pursuing it until it has been totally eradicated. The world will only be safer for our children if we start the process now.
- The public should be aware that different government agen-

cies have different agendas and different definitions of what constitutes terrorism. The public must also allow more time for facts to be established and evidence gathered before coming to their own conclusions.

- The United States, and other countries actively fighting terror, must establish international standards to determine the parameters and definition of acts of terror in a realistic way—one that takes into account the identities of the target and the perpetrator. They must establish uniform codes of acceptable law enforcement behavior in the presence of terrorists.

RESPONSES TO TERROR

Question 13:
What is the best response to terror?

ANSWER: Search and destroy.

ANALYSIS: We should have no illusions—wherever it exists, the only response to terror is to rip it out at the roots. It is essential to take action before an attack, and not to wait until after the destruction and devastation has happened to respond. It is necessary to keep up-to-date and current with active terrorists and known organizations. Know who they are and where they are and their preferred methods of operation—but expect changes.

Be proactive. When you strike, strike hard and fast. Terrorism is the greatest threat facing Western civilization today. At this stage in history nothing is more dangerous to the values held as sacrosanct by the West than terror.

Terror will not go away of its own accord. Terrorists will not wake up one day and reconsider their ways or repent. In some countries, terror is actually cultivated by those in power to deflect the attention of their citizens from their own stagnant, unresponsive governance.

Terror must be identified, sought out, and destroyed.

Question 14:
Must the response to terror be military? Isn't there an alternative way to fight terror?

ANSWER: Education is an invaluable tool in the fight against terror—but it must be used hand in hand with law enforcement, military, and judicial measures.

ANALYSIS: In the short term, the war against terror can only be fought and won with might. In the long term, the options are wider.

To win the long-term war against terror we need to develop an entirely new world view, one where people are taught to resolve their differences by negotiation and mediation, not by threatening, killing, and destroying. That can only be accomplished through an educational campaign that honors and respects differences across the board.

Societies that embrace terror must be re-oriented to realize that there are acceptable and unacceptable ways of achieving goals. The radical, fundamentalist, and violent Wahhabi denomination of Islam is the dominant creed in Saudi Arabia and Wahhabi doctrine is taught in Saudi state schools. As Mohamed Charfi, a former minister of education in Tunisia wrote in the *New York Times:* "Osama bin Laden, like the fifteen Saudis who participated in the criminal operations of September 11, seems to have been the pure product of his schooling."

In 2002, reports came out that showed that at summer camps for Palestinian children, some funded by terrorist organizations such as *Hamas* and Islamic *Jihad*, others by UNICEF, children were encouraged to learn how to play a role in terrorist attacks and how to shoot guns, and were given instruction in how to blow up Israeli buses and settlements. Suicide bombers were glorified, and a number of camp groups were named after them. Palestinian children play at being martyrs (*shaheedin*—see Question 29) the way others play Cowboys and Indians. This play is even encouraged in the kindergartens of Palestinian children.

Acts of terror will diminish only after systems of education that condone and even glorify terror are dismantled. In reality, the great strength of the West is its education. Terrorists are afraid of education that teaches co-existence and understanding of others. They know that educated populations will revolt against their rule and their methods of operation.

Re-education can work, but it is a long, slow process. We are several generations away.

Question 15:
Which is more dangerous, weapons of mass destruction or terrorism?

ANSWER: Terror is more dangerous. Weapons of mass destruction can fall into the hands of terrorists.

ANALYSIS: The biggest worry about weapons of mass destruction (WMD) is what happens if they fall into the wrong hands—and those are the hands of terrorists. Terrorists will spend vast amounts of money to procure weapons or weapon components from unstable governments. In countries with weak governments or governments in transition to democracy, it is often the case that weapons manufacturers 'lose' their stock—it is stolen by disreputable people who then sell it to the highest bidders. The highest bidders are terrorist organizations, and despotic regimes that support terrorist acts.

After the fall of the former Soviet Union numerous suitcase bombs were discovered to be missing. They had been sold on the illegal weapons market, and some were snatched up by terrorist organizations. This information came to light after the arrest of a terrorist in Egypt—the details were found on his laptop.

In addition to missing suitcase bombs, it became clear that the former Soviet Union, as it reshuffled towards democracy, had failed to properly monitor its weapons inventories. Many government employees, and even high-ranking military personnel, supplemented their meager salaries by selling weapons parts and radioactive materials to arms dealers who sold them on to the highest bidders.

Question 16:
Are Western governments powerless against the threat of terror?

ANSWER: No. Not if they act decisively against terror.

ANALYSIS: Up until 9/11 terrorists had it good; their situation was practically ideal. Most people and most governments believed that fighting terror only caused more terror. Appeasement was their answer.

Terror attacks were unexpected, unanticipated, surreal events that were seen in the movies, not in your own backyard. Terrorists were able to do what they wanted, wherever they chose, with relative impunity. Terrorists were more or less free to act in most Western democracies, and because Western countries embrace freedom, the terrorists could live their lives and carry out their plans and missions in relative anonymity and safety. The hard part was getting into the country, not the operating from within once there. Once terrorists infiltrated the United States they were under the radar. Once inside, most terrorists were "sleeping"—gathering intelligence and reporting back to the organization whose work they were doing.

Professor Sami Al-Arian, who taught computer science at Florida University, founded and served as president of a non-profit organization, the Islamic Committee for Palestine, also known as the Islamic Concern Project (ICP). ICP hosted conferences in support of the Palestinian Islamic *Jihad* terror organization. He also established a think tank called "The World and Islam Studies Enterprises" under the auspices of the university, and hired his brother in law, Ramadan Abdullah Shallah to run it. Shallah then went on to become the leader of Palestinian Islamic *Jihad*. After years of such open activity, federal officials finally indicted Al-Arian in 2002.

The fight waged by Western democracies against terrorism is made more difficult because other, non-Western countries—like Iraq,

Iran, Sudan, and Libya—harbor terrorists and terrorist masterminds. The fact that a number of known terrorists have been released from European prisons or have been conveniently 'lost' on their way to trial is extremely disturbing. The outcome of the hijacking of the Achille Lauro luxury cruise liner in 1985, in which an elderly American Jewish man was murdered, is a perfect example.

After the hijacking, the hijackers were flown off to freedom on an Egypt Air flight. A US F-14 forced the plane down in Sicily and a standoff took place between the United States and the Italian forces on the ground. President Ronald Reagan and Prime Minister Bettino Craxi disagreed over who would take the hijackers and try them. Eventually they agreed that Italy would hold the hijackers but the evidence against them would be gathered in Washington. Abu Abbas, the mastermind behind the hijacking, was taken into custody with the other terrorists. He presented the Italian authorities with his Iraqi diplomatic passport, and they released him into the custody of the Iraqi embassy, on the condition that he return when requested. When charges were filed two weeks later, he had long since slipped away. Of those that remained in custody and were sentenced, Bassam al-Asker was granted parole in 1991. Ahmad Marrouf al-Assadi, another accomplice, disappeared in 1991 while on parole. And in 1996, Youssef Magied al Molqi left the Rebibbia prison in Rome on a twelve-day furlough, and did not return.

Terrorists know in advance of their operation that if they are apprehended in certain European or Arab countries they are likely to have little to fear, and even in America they can operate relatively freely, as did Sami al-Arian. However, after 9/11, the US and many allies have become far more active in rooting out terror, and actively pursuing those to whom they would have turned a blind eye previously. We are not powerless if we act decisively.

Question 17:
Should torture be used to interrogate terrorists?

ANSWER: Yes, but only if the information gained will save lives.

ANALYSIS: Outright torture is immoral. It is against international law, and in the United States it is unconstitutional.

In addition, torture has been found to be only limitedly effective. It often does not achieve the great successes one might think. When interrogating terrorists it has been discovered that indirect forms of torture are more effective at breaking the prisoner than physical violence. Sleep deprivation, light deprivation, or keeping someone in excessively cold or warm environments for extended periods are proven effective techniques. Having the prisoner sit, kneel, or stand for excessive lengths of time and limiting medical treatment are other means of torture used by certain governments today. After the United States and Pakistan captured Khaled Sheik Mohamed, the *al Qaeda*'s chief of operations and third most important person after Osama bin Laden, they withheld non-critical medical treatment from him.

Many experts say that psychological interrogations far surpass physical torture in effectiveness in breaking the prisoner and eliciting information. Playing mind games and lying to prisoners or trying to gain their confidence are all regular methods of interrogation. If the prisoner is a chain smoker, blowing smoke in their face and never letting them smoke can be an extremely effective method of gaining information. It is amazing what an addicted smoker will do to get a cigarette.

Human rights groups and advocates question many of these techniques, but often there is more at stake than the rights of one person. The most difficult scenario is the *"ticking clock"*—when you know there is a terror attack about to happen but you don't know the specifics and you know that your prisoner has knowledge that will help you prevent the attack. If you don't get the information, many people may die. At this point, the question becomes: are you permitted to use "excessive" methods, i.e. extreme physical torture, to get that crucial, potentially life-saving information? Many legal philosophers will say yes. Some still say no. There is a debate raging in academic circles over the how, when, and if of necessary or permitted torture.

Question 18:
What is targeting? Isn't that just another name for assassination?

ANSWER: Yes, targeting is a euphemism for assassination. Targeting is also known as pinpoint attacks.

ANALYSIS: There is currently an ongoing philosophical and legal debate as to whether targeting is acceptable in international law. Western forces searching out terrorists are not mafia-like hit squads. In those situations when it is impossible to capture, interrogate, and convict a sought-after terrorist, there is no choice but to target. Targeting is a last resort, but the alternative is beyond comprehension—the rising death toll of more and more innocents.

After 9/11 we know that everything must be done to prevent terrorists from fulfilling their missions. Osama bin Laden was in the crosshairs of US forces on several occasions in the 1990s, yet President Clinton made the decision not to apprehend him. The Sudanese government made several approaches to the Clinton administration in the 1990s, offering to provide them with information on bin Laden's links with *Hezbollah* and *Hamas* or even to turn him over to American authorities via Saudi Arabia, in exchange for a normal diplomatic relationship (America had imposed trade sanctions on Sudan). Clinton refused on every occasion, and even prevented them turning over information to the British, who *were* willing to deal with Sudan. How different the world would be now had Clinton taken the opportunities offered to him!

Israel has drawn a lot of criticism for its policy of targeting terrorists, but the IDF reasons that Israel is engaged in an armed conflict, and individuals who directly take part in hostilities cannot claim immunity from attack or protection as innocent civilians. On July 31, 2001, an IDF strike took place in Nablus in which the heads of the local *Hamas* Command were killed. The *Hamas* Command targeted had been responsible for a long series of lethal terrorist attacks, in which thirty-seven civilians were murdered and three hundred and seventy-six were wounded. Among these attacks was the suicide bombing of the Dolphinarium night club in Tel Aviv, which killed twenty-one Israeli teenagers.

Almost all Western democracies use some sort of targeting. They dispatch the order only when they know that there is an impending attack and their target is central to that upcoming attack. Targeting is not used as a form of vengeance or retaliation. It acts as a pre-emptive strike.

Question 19:

If we are willing to target terrorists, what makes us different from the terrorist? Isn't killing, killing?

ANSWER: There is a very big and important difference. A pre-emptive strike is moral by most philosophical standards.

ANALYSIS: Searching out and targeting terrorists is an act of self-defense—a pre-emptive strike. Under normal circumstances, targeting does create certain legal and philosophical problems. American values like due process and being innocent until proven guilty are ignored when policies are adopted in which terrorists and terrorist infrastructures are actively searched out and destroyed.

What we must understand is that when we deal with terrorists we are not operating under normal circumstances. During wartime, the President and Congress have the power to suspend certain fundamental values for certain times regarding certain people. The laws of war also apply to conflicts with illegal combatants—those who violate the rules of battle—i.e. terrorists. The *Taliban* and *al Qaeda* are illegal combatants, as are all terrorist organizations.

The philosophical issues and questions remain, but as long as acts of terror and the murder of innocents continue we are at war with terrorists, and we must operate according to the rules of war.

Terrorists are trying to destroy democracy. America is trying to make the world safer. Life and liberty are still the American way.

Question 20:
How do you convince a pacifist to fight terror with force?

ANSWER: Give them the facts. Fighting terror is an act of self-defense!

ANALYSIS: It is only a minority of pacifists who say that pacifism should be upheld in any circumstances, and in those circumstances they themselves are prepared to die for their belief rather than fight. They would rather be killed by terrorists than raise their hands against them. However, most pacifists believe that while peaceful interaction is a duty, this must be weighed against the violation of that peace by criminals or other dangerous people, in which case the reasonable use of force is permitted, and is a form of self-defense. Terrorists definitely fit into this category.

The only good defense against terrorism is to search the terrorists out before they search you out. Otherwise, it's just too late. Partnered with the military response must also always come non-violent responses to terror. These responses include: isolation, financial investigations, prosecutions, the pursuit of all those suspected to have aided the terrorist and terrorist causes, and most importantly, education and re-education.

The pacifist might not be thoroughly convinced, but without the search for and targeting of terrorists, other non-violent responses against terror are useless. Terrorists don't ask for your individual political or religious belief before they attack. Terrorists don't discriminate.

Conclusions

- The only way to respond to terror is to destroy it. Do not—as people, as law-abiding countries or governments—be afraid to strike at the heart of terror.
- Societies that embrace terror must be re-oriented to realize that there are acceptable and unacceptable ways of achieving goals. Terrorists are afraid of education that teaches co-existence and the understanding of others. Start thinking about the process of re-education in non-Western countries. Methods must be used that are appropriate to their culture and customs, not ours.
- Use intelligence resources to infiltrate arms dealer consortiums. Arms are limited in numbers and the dealers don't care to whom they sell them. Stable governments and non-terrorist-supporting governments need to buy up the materials so that the arms and their components are off the market and away from the hands of terrorists.
- Terror can be beaten if Western countries work together. An international united front must be created. Member countries must work together and share information and intelligence in order to crack down on, arrest, interrogate, and prosecute terrorists.
- Using torture to interrogate terrorists is a sensitive issue. International, legal guidelines are important, but the ramifications of a particular circumstance and the need for vital information must also be given strong consideration.
- Targeting terrorists is a form of pre-emptive strike that saves innocent lives. Target the ringleaders; take away their ability to move freely around the world. Let the terrorists themselves sense fear.
- An entirely new policy and set of standards must be created

to deal with the fight against terror. Terrorists must not be allowed to use the freedoms of America to shelter themselves and further their terrorist causes.

- Keep up the pressure on governments that support terror. Make certain that the non-violent elements of the attack on terror are emphasized.

ISLAMIC TERROR

Question 21:
Are all terrorists Muslims?

ANSWER: All terrorists are not Muslims. But many terrorists are.

ANALYSIS: Terrorism is not limited to one group of people, or one religion, or even one region. There are many terrorist groups in the world—the partial list at the back of this book shows the wide range of active terrorist groups. Having said that, it is true that a very high proportion of terror attacks in the last few decades have been perpetrated by Muslims or by people trained by Muslim terrorists.

Islam is a monotheistic religion like Christianity and Judaism, and like them it has a long and complicated history. It has its moderates, and it has its extremists. It has elements which could be used to support terrorism, and elements that oppose it. There are over one billion Muslims in the world and, comparatively speaking, only a handful of Muslim terrorists. Many Muslims may sympathize with the terrorists and their goals but the vast majority of Muslims are upstanding citizens of their respective countries.

To understand modern Islamic terrorism, it is necessary to understand Islamic and Arab history, and Muslim attitudes to the rest of the world, and how those are perceived by extremists. The next few questions will go into these areas in more detail so that a fuller picture of the phenomenon of Islamic terror will emerge.

Question 22:
What is the traditional attitude of Islam towards the West?

ANSWER: Traditionally, Islam has been tolerant towards minorities within Islamic lands, but has felt contempt for foreign, or what they term 'infidel' culture. When infidel culture flourishes, Muslims have felt great resentment towards it.

ANALYSIS: In the 7th century, Mohammed created a new monotheistic religion, Islam, that saw itself as the final revelation of the divine truth following and replacing the partial truths of Judaism and Christianity. This religion was embraced by the Arabs, and in an astoundingly quick process, they conquered the entire Middle East and North Africa, and even made significant inroads into European territory. For many centuries, Muslim culture was the most advanced in the world. Muslim countries were far more tolerant of the minorities in their midst than were Christian countries. Islamic governments tolerated the practice, although not the preaching, of other monotheistic religions. They preserved much of the ancient classical culture of Greece and Rome at a time when Western Europe was enduring a low period of barbarism now termed the Dark Ages. They produced the Golden Age of Moorish Spain (10th and 11th centuries), during what we call the Middle Ages, a period when scientific discoveries and liberal ideas and thoughts were shared between communities and cultures within parts of the Muslim world. Muslims were more powerful, more educated, more artistic, and more scientific than their Christian contemporaries.

These accomplishments were seen by Muslims as just and appropriate for their belief in the 'true' faith: the evident superiority of the Muslim world was a Divine reward for their belief in God's revelation to Mohammed. Despite their openness to some aspects of ancient learning, the Muslim world traditionally looked at Christendom with contempt, seeing them as weak and inferior infidels. In medieval times, the only non-Muslim texts that were translated into Arabic were those dealing with medicine, astronomy, chemistry, physics, mathematics, and some philosophy—no literature or history of other countries. There was no interest in the culture of Christendom.

The turning point of Muslim expansion came in 732, when the Arab armies were turned back at Poitiers, only 180 miles from Paris. This began the *Reconquista*, a gradual re-conquest in which Christian countries not only gained back land they had lost, such as Sicily and Spain, but even made inroads into Arab lands, including the attempts by the Crusaders to conquer the Holy Land. After the European Renaissance and Enlightenment, European culture blossomed and began the scientific, military, and humanistic development that has kept it at the forefront of the modern world until today. By the eighteenth and nineteenth centuries, countries that had formerly been beneath notice were conquering the heartland of the Arab empire. The lands that weren't theirs already before World War 1 became so afterwards, when the Turkish Muslim Ottoman Empire was dismantled and parceled out to the English and French allies to administer. For a culture that was used to seeing itself as superior, this was shocking and humiliating. In every way—military, scientific, and technological—the Western world was now proving itself to be superior, when a few hundred years earlier the reverse had been the case.

The West today is the heir to European Christendom, and is viewed as such by the Arab world. For those bent on restoring the former glory of the Arab empire, the West is viewed as the enemy, just as Christendom was. This attitude goes a long way to explaining the resentment felt towards the West in much of the Arab world today.

Question 23:
Is there something in Islam that turns people into terrorists?

ANSWER: Yes and no. Islamic teachings are shaped by perception and by teachers.

ANALYSIS: Every nation goes through periods of expansion and contraction—Europe has done so as much as the Arab empire. The Crusaders were just as eager to kill Muslims in the Middle Ages as Muslim extremists today are eager to kill infidels. Many moderate Muslims do not feel threatened by the modern world and see its advantages and freedoms positively. However, extremist Muslims such as fundamentalist Islamists and pan-Arabists see the current world situation as a calamity and urge extreme measures to improve the situation of the Arab world. They may have different opinions as to why the Arab world fell from its place at the forefront of civilization, but both ideologies are united in their goal of reinstating the Arab world to its former glory.

Muslim fundamentalists see the failure of the Arab world—its poverty and backwardness—as a result of a failure to follow Islam properly. They believe that the entire world should be '*dar al Islam*'—under the rule of Islamic authority—and they believe that this can be accomplished through *jihad*. They blame Islamic rulers for being spineless and weak and kowtowing to Western powers. They see them as betrayers of the true faith, and advocate a return to fundamentals as the only cure.

The fundamentalist view of the Islamic religion is a narrow and violent one, which embraces all the xenophobic attitudes to be found in Islam, and none of the tolerant attitudes which at times were prevalent. Osama bin Laden is one such fundamentalist. Fundamentalist attitudes are fostered by certain countries and education systems, such as the Saudi Arabian Wahhabi schools, and by political leaders, and certain religious leaders.

Pan-Arabists believe in one overarching Arab empire that should not be divided into the many states and countries that now exist. When France and England gained control of the Middle East after World War I, they arbitrarily divided the region up into many different states, creating new 'countries' and installing members of tribes friendly to the allies to rule them. This created artificial monarchies and borders, the very concept of which were alien to Arab culture, which sees its loyalties as first to family and tribe, and then to the Arab people as a whole, rather than to monarchs or states. The Pan-Arabists resent the West and Western culture, and their nationalism demands the dismantling of the current borders and the unification of the Arab people into a single superpower. This would of course mean overthrowing the current monarchies, which are seen as puppets of the West. General Muammar Qaddafi of Libya is, and Saddam Hussein of Iraq was, a leader inspired by such ideas.

All Muslim terrorists fall into one of these categories, and often terrorists from different ideologies work together to destroy a common enemy, whether it is an Arab government they hope to overthrow, or a Western target they want to destroy.

Question 24:
What is the traditional Muslim attitude towards war?

ANSWER: There are many sources within the Koran that exhort the faithful to fight for their religion. There is a history of conquest within the Muslim world just as there is in the Christian world. It is the extremists today that focus on the warring aspect of their religion, not the entire Muslim world.

ANALYSIS: When Islam emerged in the Arabian desert more than 1,400 years ago, the prevailing atmosphere was one of chaos, hedonism, and polytheism. In this climate of inequity and idolatry, Islam brought a revolutionary message of equality, justice, and peace, but the prophet Mohammed had to fight to establish his faith against the Meccan establishment and other Arab tribes. The Koran and *hadith* (collected accounts about Mohammed and his teachings) reflect this reality, with an emphasis on fiery references to war, exhortations to fight oppression, and mandates to mobilize against the enemy.

In the eyes of Islam the world is divided into two—*dar al Islam* and *dar al harb*: "the world of Islam" and "the world of the sword." The world of Islam is a world filled with warmth and compassion; the world of the sword is a battlefield, filled with godlessness to be eliminated. It is this concept of insiders versus outsiders in Islam that is ripe for intolerance and that advocates the elimination of the enemy. It can lead to defining all others, i.e. unbelievers, as a threat. From there stems the need to attack unbelievers by any means necessary—including deception, lying, and even entering into false peace treaties. It was Mohammed himself who laid this foundation of making peace with an enemy in order to attack later at a more favorable time. In 628, Mohammed made a 'peace treaty' with the Qoresh tribe in Mecca so that Muslims could gain access to worship at the *Ka'abah* (according to Islamic tradition, the house built by Abraham for the sole worship of God). Two years later, when he was considerably stronger, he revoked the treaty and attacked the people of Qoresh, slaughtering every male among them. This precedent was continued by Saladin, the great Muslim warrior of the 12th century whose capture of Jerusalem in 1187 sparked the Third Crusade. Saladin is renowned for the 'peace' which he made with the Crusaders, before attacking them with such ferocity that he succeeded in driving them from the Holy Land. This is referred to frequently by leaders such as Yasser Arafat, who has said repeatedly in Arabic to the Palestinians that he is making 'the peace of Saladin' with Israel.

This is not to say that Islam is a purely warrior-like religion. Although there has been a history of warfare between Islam and their traditional enemy, Christendom, there are many Muslim countries and Muslim citizens of Western countries who follow precepts of peace which are also inherent in Islam, and do not seek out wars. The Koran states "Fight in the way of God against those who fight against you, but do not commit aggression," (Koran 2:190–2).

The problem is that there are many texts within Islam that can be used and twisted by extremists to justify their terrorist actions as righteous and holy war against infidels.

Terrorists regularly ignore the Koranic injunction against killing non-combatants.

Question 25:
What is *jihad*?

ANSWER: *Jihad* means holy war.

ANALYSIS: The root meaning of *"jihad"* is "endeavor" or "strive" or "struggle." Most of the conquest stage of Islam came within the first hundred and fifty years of its expansion, during which time *jihad* was considered to be holy war, bringing Islam to the infidel. After that time, war was not universally pursued, but selectively pursued. In many cases, war was unfeasible—the Muslims made no effort to reconquer Spain after 1492, for example—and the idea of *jihad* as holy war began to recede, to be replaced by the mystical idea of introspection and self-improvement, fighting an internal battle against the evil within yourself rather than external battles against infidels. *Jihad* was understood as a form of personal repentance that is supposed to move you back onto the right and just path.

Despite the fact that *jihad* is not one of the five pillars of the Muslim faith, the Wahhabi sect that appeared at the beginning of the 18th century elevated it to a central obligation of Islam, and reemphasized the meaning of *jihad* as military struggle. This has been taken up by all Muslim fundamentalists today as the only meaning of *jihad*, although apologists for terror will regularly say that they are referring to the peaceful introspective meaning of *jihad*.

In an interview with CNN in March 1997, Osama bin Laden declared that "we have declared *jihad* against the United States, because in our religion it is our duty to make *jihad* so that God's word is the one exalted to the heights and so that we drive the Americans away from all Muslim countries." When Yasser Arafat calls for a *jihad* to "march on Jerusalem" he is not shouting for a campaign of mass introspection. In a speech at a Johannesburg mosque he exhorted his followers to "come and fight and to start the *jihad* to liberate Jerusalem... no, it is not their capital. It is our capital...We are in need of you as Muslims, as warriors of *jihad*..."

Syrian textbooks for fourth graders preach *jihad* as an obligation: "The believers, the *jihad* warriors, sold their souls to *Allah*.... They were killed for the cause of *Allah* and became eternal martyrs. Therefore they are worthy of *Allah*'s Paradise."

When Muslim clerics call for every believer to "rise up in *jihad*" against the West, they are not issuing a call for Muslim mass repentance. The Washington Times in October 2002 quoted Sheikh Mohammed Saleh Al-Munajjid from a sermon on *jihad* saying: "Muslims must educate their children to *jihad*... This is the greatest benefit of the situation: educating the children to *jihad* and to hatred of the Jews, the Christians, and the infidels; educating the children to *jihad* and to revival of the embers of *jihad* in their souls. This is what is needed now." Calls such as these are mustering forces for holy war—for terrorism.

Jihad is the calling of most terrorists today.

Question 26:
Who becomes a terrorist? Why?

ANSWER: Murderers who kill to make their point.

ANALYSIS: It is a mistake to think that terrorists are poor or uneducated and therefore acting out of hopelessness and desperation. In recent years, many of those involved in terror attacks have been well-educated and from upper middle class, wealthy families. These perpetrators of terror are committed to their terrorist cause whether it is political or religious.

Not long ago there was a very simple profile fitting nearly every Muslim terrorist. They were young, male, poor, uneducated, and from one of a handful of areas from several specific countries, typically Libya, Sudan, Lebanon, Syria, Iraq, and Afghanistan.

Over the recent decades that profile has changed. Today the profile includes women, fathers, people over thirty years old, and those who are educated and rich. Some of the hijackers of 9/11 met while studying at university. Osama bin Laden is the scion of an extremely wealthy Saudi family. His father established one of Saudi Arabia's leading business and construction conglomerates (the Bin Laden Group) and he grew up living a life of luxury.

Some terrorists believe and are taught that they will receive a place in heaven and seventy virgins by murdering those they see as heretics and infidels. Others believe that it is the only way to pursue their political cause. Sheik Raid Salah, leader of the Islamic movement in Israel, gave an interview to the newspaper *Ha'aretz* on October 26, 2001 in which he stated "It is written in the Koran and in the Sunna (the tradition and the life of Muhammad), the *shaheed* [(martyr)] receives from Allah six special things, including seventy virgins, no torment in the grave, and the choice of seventy members of his family and confidants to enter paradise with him."

Question 27:
What are homicide or suicide bombers?

ANSWER: People who rig their bodies or cars with a bomb, with the objective of killing as many people as possible while also killing themselves.

ANALYSIS: The terms are synonyms. Some people prefer to use the term homicide bomber because using the word 'suicide' sounds more sympathetic to the bomber, and also ignores the fact that these terrorists do not see themselves as committing suicide but as martyrs.

Terrorist handlers have concluded that suicide bombing is an efficient and accurate method of attack. It is better than planting an explosive and triggering it by remote control. When worn or carried by a suicide terrorist, the bomb explodes right in the heart of a crowd, and is harder to detect.

Most suicide bombers are volunteers. Handlers train the terrorists, teaching them how to operate the bomb and where to go and how to most effectively attack. They are also taught that should they be caught, or if they are surrounded because they look suspicious, they should immediately blow themselves up, even if alone, in order to avoid capture. This is so that they will not be vulnerable to interrogation and give away vital details about their commanders. This idea, of aborting the plan and killing only yourself, has discouraged many suicide bombers while in training.

These terrorists are not drugged or brainwashed. They are fervent believers in their cause—whether it is religious or political. Handlers play on the weaknesses of their recruits. If the recruit is religiously motivated, handlers emphasize the religious obligation to be a martyr. If the recruit is politically oriented, they emphasize the importance of being a soldier for their nation and their people. An Egyptian volunteer who travelled to Iraq to be a suicide bomber against the Americans, in March 2003, said in an interview with *Al Jazeera*, the Arab satellite TV channel, that his was a "God-blessed martyrdom-seeking mission.... We seek God's satisfaction. We seek victory first, and martyrdom in the cause of God second. God will take care of [my children], and anyone who is taken care of by God will not be forgotten."

Islamic males become suicide bombers believing they will be rewarded in heaven, and knowing that their families will be well paid for their acts. In the past, the Saudis, the Iraqis, the Iranians, and the Palestinian Authority have all put up money for the support of the families of suicide bombers. In 2002, A Western journalist was in the town of Tulkarm, in the West Bank, and witnessed the process when forty-seven families of suicide bombers were each given $25,000 from Saddam Hussein's checkbook, via a Palestinian official.

Suicide bombers do not see themselves as ending their lives, but as moving on to a higher stage. The *New York Times* reported that part of the training of a suicide bomber involves watching broadcasts of films of a dead boy beckoning the trainee to join him in paradise. On June 7, 2001 the *Hamas* newspaper *Al Risala* published the will of Said al Hutari, the suicide bomber who killed twenty-one teenagers at the Dolphinarium nightclub in Tel Aviv. It reads, "I will turn my body into bombs that will hunt the sons of Zion, blast them and burn their remains. Call out in joy Oh my mother, distribute sweets Oh my father and brothers, a wedding with the black-eyed virgin awaits your son in paradise."

Question 28:

How can parents of suicide bombers take so much pride in the death of their child after he or she has murdered so many innocent people?

ANSWER: Parents of suicide bombers see their children as heroes and martyrs, not as murderers.

ANALYSIS: It takes an entirely different mindset to begin to understand how a parent can see a child who has just killed themselves and murdered many innocent others as a national hero, but the parents are as convinced by the ideology of the bombers as the terrorists themselves. They see their children as martyrs and heroes.

Parents of suicide bombers take tremendous pride in the actions of their children. Suicide bombers bring honor and fame to their families and their communities. The parents have newfound status and, as mentioned earlier, even receive large amounts of money from governments supportive of terrorist activities.

Some parents even go so far as to publicly proclaim that they wished all of their children would grow up to be martyrs too. Hassan al Hutari, the father of the bomber mentioned in the previous question, who killed twenty-one teenagers, told the Associated Press, "'I am very happy and proud of what my son did and I hope all the men of Palestine and Jordan would do the same." Paid death announcements of suicide bombers in newspapers resemble wedding announcements. The Palestinian paper *Al Istiglal* published an announcement on October 4, 2001 which read: "with great pride the Palestine Islamic *Jihad* marries a member of its military wing, the martyr Yossuf al Adhami to the black-eyed virgin."

Question 29:
What is a *shaheed*?

ANSWER: A martyr.

ANALYSIS: According to Islam, a *shaheed*, literally "a witness," is a person who dies while performing *jihad*. Because of this action, the *shaheed* is transformed into a martyr in this world and elevated directly to heaven in the next world.

While this concept has always been present in Islam, like the concept of *jihad*, it has been adaptable, so that when *jihad* was emphasized as a spiritual battle, a scholar or someone who led prayer services could be praised as a *shaheed*. A cult of martyrdom developed during the Iran-Iraq war in the early 1980s. There were so many fatalities in the war that the idea of the *shaheed* as martyr began to saturate Iran's religious institutions in order to encourage enough young men to fight. This concept continued and spread throughout the Arab world through fundamentalist preaching and education. The common concept today is that anyone who dies in the act of attacking Islam's enemies, whomever they are perceived to be—specifically Jews and Westerners—is lauded as a *shaheed*.

Every hijacker on 9/11 was a *shaheed*. The terrorist who murdered teenagers at a disco in Tel Aviv is a *shaheed*. The terrorist who drove his truck into the US Marine barracks in Beirut, Lebanon in 1983, murdering 290 US marines is a *shaheed*. Sheik Abd al Halim Ayyash of Jerusalem said in 2001, "a *shaheed* has high rank and value in Islam, in both this world and the hereafter. To strive for martyrdom is a desired virtue in Islam."

Question 30:
What does Islam say about suicide?

ANSWER: Suicide is absolutely forbidden in Islam.

ANALYSIS: It may come as a surprise, but Islam rejects suicide. Life is held to be sacred, and suicide is one of the most grievous sins one can perform against God.

According to the teachings of Islam, taking one's life is the ultimate act of selfishness. Islam teaches that only *Allah* has the right to take human life. The Koran, Islam's holy text, records that the teachings of the prophet Mohammad clearly reject suicide. In addition, the *Shariyah* (Islamic law) emphasizes time after time the prohibition against suicide. Here are several examples:

"And whoever commits suicide with a piece of iron will be punished with the same piece of iron in the Hell Fire." Jundab the Prophet narrated: "A man was inflicted with wounds and he committed suicide, and so *Allah* said: My slave has caused death on himself hurriedly, so I forbid Paradise for him." (*Sahih Bukhari 2.445*)

"Allah's Messenger said: none amongst you should make a request for death, and do not call for it before it comes, for when any of you dies, he ceases (to do good) deeds and the life of a believer is not prolonged but for goodness." (*Hadith—Muslim #6485*)

That's why Islamic terrorists, who are often fervently religious, see themselves as martyrs, never as suicides. They do not see themselves as violating Islamic law. They see themselves as fulfilling a religious obligation, and defending Islam and their God.

Question 31:
Who are the *fedayeen*?

ANSWER: In Arabic, *fedayeen* means 'Men of Sacrifice.' We call them terrorists; they see themselves as warriors of God.

ANALYSIS: The *fedayeen,* or *fedai,* are Muslim soldiers fighting the enemy. *Fedayeen* assume their responsibilities with the understanding that they will die in the fight. They are the Muslim equivalent of Japan's kamikaze fighters.

The original *fedayeen* were 11th century assassins who pledged their allegiance to their founder and leader Hassan ben Sabbah. Today's *fedayeen* are fighters against the West. In today's Muslim world a terrorist fighter, while still alive, is known as a *fedayeen*. After death, the *fedayeen* becomes a martyr, a *shaheed*.

Not so ironically, Saddam Hussein chose to name his private military wing *Fedayeen*. They were soldiers in plain clothes who intimidated Iraqi civilians.

Conclusions

- It is important to know more about the history and culture of Islam, its ideals and how it interacts with other cultures and peoples. For most people it will be impossible to learn the religious book of Islam—the Koran—in the original Arabic, but it is possible to find and read good translations and historical works on Islam. (See the recommended reading suggestions at the back of this book.)
- Extremists exist in every religion. Extremists often twist the words of the Koran to justify their actions against civilians. Islamic sources have strict rules governing warfare that are broken by terrorists claiming to act in God's name.
- There is a moderate side to Islam. Support moderate Muslim leaders and encourage Muslim leaders and historians to educate their community and emphasize the alternate meanings of *jihad* and martyrdom. Create a propaganda campaign that exposes true Islamic tradition, which holds that those who kill themselves and non-combatants are murderers and suicides, and not martyrs. Clerics are among the best professionals to organize and implement these campaigns.
- The funding and encouragement of extremism can be stopped. Stopping the money to families of suicide bombers will remove a large degree of the incentive.

SPONSORS OF TERROR

Question 32:
What is the link between despots and terrorism?

ANSWER: Despots support terror.

ANALYSIS: The relationship between despots and terrorists is a symbiotic, mutually beneficial one. Despots support terrorists by giving them refuge and headquarters in their countries, giving them money for their operations, training, and weapons. In return, the terrorists carry out much of the dirty work of despots, and even train their regular forces, so that they can maintain their own images of dubious propriety. Terrorists also get positive reinforcement from these despotic leaders of rogue nations; the belief that their acts of terror are done for a higher calling, on behalf of a larger, more important cause, is strengthened because it is supported by a government.

The governments of Syria, Libya, Sudan, and Iran provide a safe haven and safety net for terrorist organizations and operatives, keeping the terrorists far from the waiting arms of international justice. Saddam Hussein's Iraq did the same. The next two questions deal separately with the cases of Iran and Iraq, but a few examples of the terrorist activities of the other countries are worth mentioning here.

Sudan is a Wahhabi-style regime, like Saudi Arabia, and participates in the fundamentalism of that movement. Osama bin Laden spent half of the 1990s in Sudan, financing terrorists throughout the region and working directly with the Sudanese government to create terrorist camps. Syria directly sponsors the terrorist group *Hezbollah* together with Iran, and the terrorist groups Popular Front for the Liberation of Palestine and Palestinian Islamic *Jihad* have their headquarters in Damascus, gaining training, weapons, safe haven, and logistical support from the Syrians. In the 1980s, the Kurdistan

Workers' Party used Syria as a headquarters and base of operations against neighboring Turkey. Libya has provided support and training not only for Palestinian terrorists, but also for the IRA, the Basque separatists, and Sierra Leone's Revolutionary United Front. Experts on the region have implicated Libya in backing plots to assassinate the presidents of Chad, Egypt, Sudan, Tunisia, and Zaire. The most infamous terrorist attack that Libya is responsible for was the 1988 bombing of Pan Am Flight 103 over Lockerbie, Scotland, which killed 270 people. In 2001, a Scottish court convened in the Netherlands convicted Libyan intelligence agent Abdul Basset al-Megrahi for murder, for his role in the bombing.

The despot and the terrorist share styles of leadership. They embrace tyranny and fear as methods of controlling people. The despotic leader does to his people what the terrorist hopes to do to the West. The tools are slightly different, and the despots carry a thin veneer of legitimacy that the terrorists lack, but the mindset and cruelty and disregard for human life are the same.

Question 33:
What was Saddam Hussein's role in terror?

ANSWER: He paid the families of suicide bombers and supported terrorist activities both financially and morally.

ANALYSIS: Saddam Hussein supported terrorist organization by providing funding, intelligence, training, refuge, and even weapons for terrorists around the world. Saddam used terrorists to threaten the countries around him and Israel. He funded, trained, and sheltered the *Muhahedin-e Jhala*, a group that operates against Iran, and has supported most of the major terrorist organizations that operate against Israel. Abu Nidal, one of the most infamous world terrorists until bin Laden, was recently assassinated in Iraq, where he had been making his home for many years. Another infamous terrorist, Abu Abbas, chose Baghdad as his home.

Saddam rewarded the families of suicide bombers with checks for $25,000 in order to provide incentive for young people to kill themselves and murder others. He gave a lesser amount if something went wrong in the attack and the terrorist was only wounded. If a 'work accident' occurred while assembling the bomb or transferring it to its location, the families still received money, but again it was a lesser amount.

Saddam's intelligence service had contacts with *al Qaeda* in Sudan, and although it is unproven, it is highly likely he played a role in the 1993 World Trade Center bombing. In April 2001, only five months before 9/11, Mohammed Atta, the lead hijacker, met with an Iraqi intelligence agent named al-Ani who was working undercover as secretary and consul in the Iraqi embassy in Prague. Two weeks later, $100,000 was transferred to Atta's bank account in Florida. Since the war with Iraq, secret Iraqi intelligence documents have been discovered in Baghdad that have provided the first concrete evidence of a direct link between *al Qaeda* and Saddam Hussein's regime.

Saddam Hussein was also not averse to perpetrating his own personal acts of terror. He used chemical weapons against his own citizens and against Iranians, and vicious torture and executions were used against his enemies. In one of the worst single mass killings in recent history, in 1988 he dropped mustard gas and nerve toxins on the Kurdish Iraqi city of Halabja, killing over 5,000 people, mostly civilians.

Question 34:
How is Iran connected to terror?

ANSWER: Iran is directly connected to terror, supplying weapons, guns, explosives, and training to the terrorists.

ANALYSIS: Iran has been a sponsor of terror for decades. Iran is responsible for fueling, funding, and supporting directly and indirectly almost every extremist Islamic terrorist group. Unlike some terror-supporting regimes, Iran has not hidden its sponsorship of terrorism. Along with supplying weapons to terrorist groups around the world, Iran sponsors *Hezbollah*, *Hamas* and the *Islamic Jihad* in Lebanon, Egypt, and in Gaza.

In 1992, the Iranians blew up the Israeli Embassy in Buenos Aires, Argentina, killing twenty-seven people and injuring hundreds. Two years later, Iran was responsible for the blowing-up of the Jewish Community Center, also in Buenos Aires. Eighty-five people were murdered and hundreds injured when a car bomb detonated and destroyed the building. In March 2003, an Argentinean High Court Judge released a four hundred page legal ruling issuing arrest warrants against the Iranians who executed the terror attack. The warrants were issued against the head of Iranian secret intelligence (who was also the Iranian cultural attaché in Buenos Aires) and the former minister of education. Interpol was asked to make the arrests. Also present at the planning meeting that devised the two bombing attacks in Argentina was the current, supposedly liberal, Prime Minister of Iran, Mohammad Khatami.

Iranian arms shipments to terrorists are sometimes intercepted. The best example of this is the Karin-A, a huge ship filled with all kinds of weapons and explosives, which was captured by Israel on January 3, 2002 on its way to the Palestinian Authority.

Iran has mastered the art of packing arms in airtight barrels that can be dropped offshore. The barrels sink and are then lifted up by yanking a pull-string. Divers lift the barrels out of the water and are picked-up by innocent looking fishing boats.

Iran is accumulating and manufacturing weapons and technology at an unbelievable rate. The Islamic republic is a government defined by hatred of others and is vociferous in preaching the destruction of the West.

Question 35:
Who sponsors terror?

ANSWER: Governments, rich individuals, and even the man on the street, sometimes even without his knowledge. Anyone who gives money or other support to the terrorists.

ANALYSIS: Countries like Saudi Arabia sponsor terror directly because the State school system is run along the principles of Wahhabi Islam which preaches fundamentalism, terror, and the destruction of Western civilization.

Libya, Iran, Syria, Iraq, Sudan, Yemen, and the Palestinian Authority all directly sponsor terror now or have done so in the past by allocating funds to terrorists and/or by harboring terrorists. These countries also sponsor terror by giving money to the families of suicide bombers.

Wealthy individuals, especially from Saudi Arabia, have personally contributed large sums to terrorist organizations and to the families of terrorists. Osama bin Laden is the most notable example of an individual or family who sponsors terror, but there are many others like him.

The Western world permitted and still allows some terrorist organizations to operate. Governments have given tax-free status to groups to collect charity at local mosques, on street corners and at universities in the United States, Canada, England, and throughout Europe. These groups often collect charitable funds under the guise of humanitarian aid to Palestinians or others in need and then funnel the money to terrorist organizations. One of the most shocking examples of this duplicity was exposed in October 2001, when NATO intelligence officers searched the Sarajevo office of the Saudi High Commissioner for Aid to Bosnia. The supposedly humanitarian institution was a front for *al Qaeda,* and an exploration of the site revealed files with photographs of terrorist targets in Washington DC with government buildings clearly marked, computer programs with instructions for using crop dusters to spread poison, pictures of *al Qaeda* targets before and after attacks, including the World Trade Center and the USS Cole, and materials for the production of fake credit cards and State Department ID badges.

Palestinian terrorists have used Red Crescent (the Muslim affiliate of the Red Cross) ambulances to transport bombers and the bomb laden belts that suicide terrorists wear.

Question 36:
Why would a country sponsor terror?

ANSWER: To keep their own hands clean and still achieve a goal that they cannot directly pursue on their own.

ANALYSIS: Countries sponsor terrorism in order to achieve national goals that they know are unacceptable to the greater world community. These countries—and they are not just despotic regimes—know that they are unable to participate directly in attacks, so instead they train terrorists, supply them with their tools, harbor them, pay them, and aid them in their escape. They also provide terrorists with insight and operational information on a level far surpassing what they could have assembled on their own. They know what happens in airports and other secure areas because their governments are privy to those security measures—their diplomats and politicians use the systems.

These countries seldom condemn a terror attack outright. They express their concern for the loss of all human life including the lives of terrorists. They justify the terror by saying that the reason for terrorist strikes is the result of the actions taken by the victims *"what do you expect after so many years of this policy or that behavior or those conditions."* They place blame on the victims, not on the terrorists or terrorist organizations.

In a December 2001 issue of the pro-Syrian Lebanese daily *Al-Safir*, President Hosni Mubarak of Egypt expressed his support of terror: "Let's be clear. Someone defending his land from within his land is not a terrorist. If I expel a colonialist from my land, how can this be called terrorism? The Lebanese youth is connected to his land, and set out to defend it, just like the Palestinian who fights and defends his land and wants it returned."

The Saudi interior minister Prince Nayef Ibn Abd Al-Aziz, outraged America when his statements on 9/11 were published in a Kuwaiti newspaper, claiming that the devastation of September 11 was a Zionist plot: "Prince Nayef stressed that relations between the Saudi and US governments are strong despite the Zionist-controlled media that manipulated the events of September 11 and turned US public opinion against Arabs and Islam. Prince Nayef said, 'we put big question marks and ask who committed the events of September 11 and who benefited from them. Who benefited from events of 11/9? (sic) I think they [the Zionists] are behind these events.'"

An extract from a letter written to the Saudi ambassador to the United States by Congressmen Peter Deutsch and Eliot Engel about these statements reads, "Comments such as these are not only an affront to our government and the international community, which have extensively documented the self-admitted culpability of Osama bin-Laden and *al-Qaeda*, but they are an insult to the three thousand families who lost loved ones in the devastating attacks. While such offensive accusations have been adopted by extremist anti-American and anti-Israel groups over the past year, these lies have not been purported by government officials of any nation. Yet despite the nature of the comments, Saudi officials have not publicly condemned the egregious remarks, Prince Nayef continues to lead your Interior Ministry, and, most outrageously, the Prince's statement has been prominently displayed on the 'Saudi Arabian Information Resource', an official Saudi Ministry of Information website."

Many Arab countries secretly applaud the actions of terrorism against the West, and use them to buy off public opinion within their own countries. That's why they support it via the back door while politely and diplomatically expressing their condolences via the front door. They say one thing in English and something very different for their countrymen and other Arab countries in Arabic.

Question 37:
How can you blame an entire country for the acts of only a few of its citizens?

ANSWER: When a country is complicit in the acts of its citizens, it too must be held accountable.

ANALYSIS: It may sound unfair to blame an entire society for the acts of a few, but as we have already seen in previous questions, in certain countries the government actually helps their citizens become terrorists. When help is received through financial support (as is the case with the Palestinian Authority) or through the support of fundamentalist educational institutions (as is the case with Saudi Arabia) those countries should be blamed.

Countries that harbor terrorists, sponsor terror, give a silent stamp of approval, or even simply turn a blind eye, bear some responsibility for the terror. Often, the citizens of these countries are also vocal in their support of terror. After an attack they dance in the streets and speak of the importance of attacking the West. They themselves may not be terrorists but they support the terrorists' acts and their results.

While the world is used to seeing Palestinians celebrate after suicide attacks that leave scores of Israelis dead, seeing them dance in the streets after 9/11 was a source of astonishment and dismay. Reading newspapers from the Arab and Muslim world and seeing how they blamed the CIA and Israel's Intelligence Service, the *Mossad*, for the terror attacks was a true eye opener for the citizens of the Unites States.

Those who allow terrorists to reside in their countries cannot be considered participants in the international fight against terror. If you're not with us, you're against us.

Question 38:
How can you convince millions of people not to support terrorists?

ANSWER: Through education and economic incentives.

ANALYSIS: As we've seen, many of the countries which support terror have a citizenry that also supports terror and hates the West. That adds up to millions of people around the world who embrace the acts of terrorists.

Terrorists receive popular support in many countries around the world for two simple reasons. The first is political—many hold the same beliefs as the terrorists, even if they are not active terrorists themselves. They believe their actions are correct. The second reason is because many of the terrorist organizations sponsor numerous social services for the masses. They provide soup kitchens and nursery schools and medical care. For example, dental care, a luxury in many parts of the world, will cost as little as $1 after you agree to send your children to schools sponsored by the terrorists and make certain your wife follows strict Islamic law in her dress code.

This support for the terrorists organizations can be subverted by investing in, and providing the goods and services the terrorists provide. In addition, by creating educational programs, children's facilities, and medical care services, the power, dependence, and monopoly that the terrorists organizations hold over their populations can be broken.

Conclusions

- Not all societies and cultures share the same values. Certain countries and leaders are duplicitous and two-faced. Governments, like their citizens, must remember that actions do indeed speak louder than words. Like Saddam's Iraq and the *Taliban* in Afghanistan, they will be held accountable for their actions.
- Countries that support terror must be exposed. International pressure must be applied to make certain that governments around the world that do support terror are not allowed to pretend that they don't.
- Iran must be isolated, and prevented from importing and exporting weapons and the scientists necessary to develop them.
- International pressure, including military action, must be brought to bear on despots to treat their citizens with proper humanity.
- Economic incentives, foreign aid, and educational programs must be used to convince leaders to re-educate their countries against murderous violence as a response to problems.
- Follow the money trail. Block all the funds of countries that support terror and confiscate the funds of people who donate and raise money for terror.
- Monitor the actions of your allies, or those who claim to be your allies, and demand consistency.
- Education about the value of human life is essential, as is education about non-violent ways to achieve change.

THE STRUCTURE
OF TERROR

Question 39:
Does the terrorist act alone?

ANSWER: Almost never.

ANALYSIS: Although there have been acts of terror perpetrated by individuals, almost all terror attacks require a large network of people who raise funds for the organization, coordinate the act, and dispatch the actual perpetrators.

Terror is like a jigsaw puzzle. Many pieces must fit together, and if a single element is missing the attack is likely to fail and therefore it is often aborted—that is why roadblocks and alerts are actually effective in fighting terror.

A typical act of terror can involve as many as fifty people, including the funders who raise the money for the attack, political and religious leaders who encourage people to support terror, recruiters who find the terrorists, planners, technicians, and engineers who work out the details and create the weapons for an attack, messengers who deliver components of the bomb or act as go-betweens, transporters who take the terrorists where they need to go, and operatives—the terrorists themselves.

We often focus on the final stage, but the person who plants a bomb or hijacks a plane or blows himself up in a crowded restaurant is by no means the only perpetrator of the attack. The whole chain is vital to the final product. Morally and legally each member of the chain in the conspiracy is guilty of mass murder. They are all terrorists.

Question 40:
Is there a difference if a person acts alone or as a group member?

ANSWER: Yes, a vast difference exists between a lone terrorist and a terrorist organization.

ANALYSIS: The more members of a terrorist organization there are, the greater the possibility of finding informants and breaking the group through infiltration. The more people involved in an attack, the greater the trail of faxes, emails, and telephone and cell-phone conversations that can be intercepted and used to find a way to prevent the attack before it happens.

By contrast, a lone terrorist is nearly impossible to stop before the fact. There is no communication, therefore there can be no leaks, and no possibility of infiltration or finding out details. The only chance of stopping somebody who acts alone, is if that person needs to buy a weapon or tools and the seller becomes suspicious, or if they exhibit suspicious behavior when scouting or researching the target which alerts authorities. Otherwise, the last chance—a faint one indeed—is that the terrorist be stopped in the middle of carrying out his act of terror.

Question 41:
Do terrorists have an ethical code?

ANSWER: Yes, terrorists have a code of behavior.

ANALYSIS: It sounds strange, almost beyond comprehension, but terrorists do live by a code.

How can mass murderers of innocent women and children have a code of ethical behavior? Terrorists want to kill as many of their enemy as possible, but in their minds they are acting out of a need to protect their own. They want their parents, family, and friends to be proud of them. They see their actions as heroic and as martyrdom, not as mass murder. That is why we often see videos the terrorists have made before their attacks, and why terrorists almost always leave behind letters and messages for their families.

Many terrorist groups are involved in social action to improve the conditions of those they are fighting to liberate, and to obtain their support. *Hamas* and *Hezbollah* provide soup kitchens, nursery schools, and hospitals for their communities.

The terrorist will do anything to achieve his mission—and that includes working with other terrorist groups, even if their goals and religious ideals are radically different. A part of their code is that they believe that "the enemy of my enemy is my friend," and so they join forces. Shi'ite Muslims believe that Alawites are deviants from the Islamic tradition, yet Iran's Ayatollah Khomeini, a devout Shi'ite, allied himself with the Syrian leader Assad, an Alawite. *Hamas* is a religious Sunni Muslim group, but has worked with the PFLP which is Marxist and secular.

Question 42:
What do we know about terrorist organizations?

ANSWER: The best we can hope to know is who their leaders are and what their causes are. We learn the rest only after the fact.

ANALYSIS: Most terrorist organizations, whether politically or religiously motivated, are proud of their agenda. They want us to know what they're fighting for, what their systems of beliefs are, and they want us to fear them—but in order to operate effectively, all other details of their organizations must be kept secret.

We usually learn of an intended target only after it has been attacked. We discover the identities of operatives only after they've blown themselves up or been heralded by their peers. We learn of their methods of attack after those methods have been used successfully.

When we are really lucky, terrorists or information about planned terrorist attacks are intercepted before the act.

Question 43:
Is there a relationship between drug trafficking and terrorism?

ANSWER: There is a deep symbiotic relationship between terror and the drug trade.

ANALYSIS: Terror requires money and weapons, and the easiest way to get both is by selling drugs. This nexus of drugs and terror now has a name—narco-terror.

The places where drugs are grown and processed are normally countries with weak governments—places where the police and the government are rife with corruption. This is especially true in Central and South America, the Middle East, the former Soviet Republics and Asia. This provides a perfect breeding ground for the terrorist who needs quick money, easily procured guns, larger weapons, and experience.

As an example, in 2000 Afghanistan produced 3,276 tons of opium, used to produce heroin, out of a worldwide total of 4,691 tons. The heroin sold on the streets of Europe and America paid for the weapons of the *Taliban* and the terrorist groups they supported.

The United Nations declaration 'Measures to Eliminate International Terrorism' was adopted at the UN General Assembly's 49th session in 1995. The declaration emphasizes the dangers of the growing marriage of convenience between drug lords and terrorists, and those who help them out—like money launderers, arms dealers and smugglers of radioactive materials.

Conclusions

- Carrying out a terror attack is a complicated process. Intelligence, informants, and common sense must be used to stop the process at every possible point. When there is one chink in the process, the entire plan fails.
- Vigilance must be observed by law enforcement agencies, intelligence organizations, and government agencies.
- Do not return the body of the suicide bomber to the family. Bury it in a criminal or prisoner's cemetery.
- The funeral of a dead terrorist must not be allowed to become a protest and a rally for those who believe in terrorist activities.
- Find other ways to provide the services that terrorist organizations provide in health, education, and welfare. Undercut their influence.
- Strengthen drug prevention and rehabilitation programs. Knock the wind out of drug traffickers. Help law enforcers defeat drug dealers in your neighborhood.

TOOLS OF TERROR

Question 44:
How much does it cost to perpetrate a terror attack?

ANSWER: As little as several hundred dollars, and as much as several hundred thousand dollars.

ANALYSIS: One of the truly frightening aspects of terror is how little it can cost to put an attack together and how many billions of dollars it takes to protect ourselves.

A successful terror attack requires little more than an automatic weapon—a relatively cheap and accessible commodity on the gun market. Old guns can be bought for as little as $50–$100, and twenty year old RPGs can be bought for only $500. A bomb can be put together with substances such as acetone, nitrogen, and fertilizers—all materials that can be bought in a hardware store for next to nothing.

Terrorists can attack even when money is scarce. When money is plentiful, the plans are usually more sophisticated, more terrorists are involved, the target is grander, and the numbers of murdered and injured are incrementally larger.

Question 45:
What is a suitcase bomb?

ANSWER: A small nuclear device.

ANALYSIS: A suitcase bomb is a small nuclear bomb that can be carried and detonated within a suitcase. It is effective because it is so easy to carry that it hardly ever arouses suspicion. It can be placed almost anywhere and left for detonation, or be detonated by a suicide bomber.

Since the bomb is small, the total physical damage it causes is also small, but since it is nuclear, the blast and the radioactive fallout is large enough to contaminate an entire city.

Since the fall of the former Soviet Union, several dozen suitcase bombs are unaccounted for. They were probably sold on the black market to the highest bidders—who are most often terrorist organizations or countries that harbor and sponsor terrorists.

Egyptian intelligence interrogated several *al Qaeda* agents and discovered that *al Qaeda* may have several suitcase bombs.

Question 46:
What is a dirty bomb?

ANSWER: A simple explosive with radioactive material in it.

ANALYSIS: Dirty bombs may be the wave of the future for terror. Making a nuclear bomb is expensive and requires serious knowledge and experience, but a dirty bomb is much simpler and only requires a few of the elements found in nuclear devices.

A 'regular' nuclear bomb creates an explosion inside an atom of uranium or plutonium. A dirty bomb puts normal explosives together with uranium or plutonium and hopes that the explosion of the normal explosives will carry radioactive fallout with it and contaminate an area significantly larger than the bomb's own strength.

Since the fall of the Soviet Union, it has been relatively easy for terrorists to get their hands on plutonium and uranium. There are always terrorist-friendly countries and individuals who (for a price) will sell small amounts that will go unnoticed because of slack or corrupt monitoring facilities.

These weapons and their components can easily be smuggled in and out of countries, especially by sea.

Question 47:
Are new weapons being developed that might fall into terrorist hands?

ANSWER: Yes, and the biggest fear with all weapons is that they might fall into the wrong hands.

ANALYSIS: Scientists have developed some wonderful weapons that reduce the numbers of casualties in war, such as smart bombs or weapons that stun without killing. These developments are major strides forward for the civilized army whose objective is to limit the loss of life of innocent victims. On the other hand, these same weapons could wreak terrible damage if they fell into the wrong hands.

One of the newest weapons available today is a microwave bomb (also known as the Electromagnetic Pulse Bomb or the ebomb). The microwave bomb does not hurt anyone directly, but it destroys all bombs and disrupts and controls all communication systems including cellphones, telephones and computers. It leaves the enemy with no ability to communicate or co-ordinate its forces, and requires all remaining weapons to be manned by hand. It's a fantastically effective weapon, that minimizes loss of life—but if it should be duplicated or stolen by terrorists the damage it could perpetrate on America and the West—totally computer-dependant societies—is unfathomable and potentially lethal.

Conclusions

- Terror must be stopped at its source. There must be a crack down on everyone involved—from illegal arms dealers to those individuals and governments who fund terror.
- The cost of terrorism must be made too high for any group of individuals to pay.
- If you see a suspicious object, report it. Move away, and keep others away.
- Accept the minor inconveniences of bag searches and metal detectors in public places. Co-operate with law enforcement guidelines and practices.
- Strict monitoring of radioactive elements complete with international intervention and controls is imperative.
- Provide financial and other incentives to atomic scientists to keep their knowledge and materials from falling into the wrong hands.
- Even stricter safeguards must be put in place to protect not only weapons but the blueprints for developing weapons.

TERRORISM
AND AMERICA

Question 48:
Why do Muslim terrorists hate the United States and other Western countries?

ANSWER: Because we symbolize everything that the Muslim terrorist abhors.

ANALYSIS: Whether you are a pan-Arabist or an Islamic fundamentalist you will see the West as the enemy and aggressor. The root of the hatred of America by Muslim terrorists lies in what was discussed in questions 22–24. Christendom originally halted the progress of Islamic conquest in the 8ᵗʰ century, and became enshrined in Muslim culture as the quintessential foe of Islam for centuries afterwards. Then the West, the heir of Christendom, became a colonizer, and at the height of the Imperialist Age, dominated the entire Arab world. When this period was over, the West split the Arab world into multiple, artificial states and installed regimes to control them, that the majority of Arabs consider to be illegitimate, weak puppets of Western powers.

While the West may perceive all these facts as now irrelevant history, they are still great objects of resentment in the Arab world. The Arab world knows that it was once at the forefront of civilization and yet has now fallen so low that not only has it not contributed anything new to world culture in centuries, but Arab culture itself has become infested with Western philosophies, science, law, and ideologies.

The West is also seen as an immoral culture of TV and sexual promiscuity which could tempt good Muslims away from the true path. The Muslim world no longer sees Christianity as simply heretical, now they see the West as godless—only caring for money and success, and having no real values. For all these reasons, the West is the natural enemy of the Muslim terrorist.

Question 49:
Do terrorists hate the United States because the United States is a friend of Israel?

ANSWER: No. That is false. Terrorists hate America and they hate Israel.

ANALYSIS: This is a common misconception, but it is wrong to think that terrorism against the United States happens because of Israel. To say that the United States and Israel are allies and close friends is correct. It is also correct to say that they share a common cause—the fight against terror.

The Palestinian issue is one that has been used to cloud the real reasons for Arab hatred of Israel, and is used constantly by terrorists as their 'reason' for acting, using it as a pretext to obfuscate their real goals. Long before there was any Palestinian question, when Israel was declared a state in 1948, five Arab armies rushed to invade and destroy it. The PLO was founded in 1964, three years *before* the 1967 war in which the Israelis took control of the West Bank and Gaza, and their charter still today calls for the destruction of the entire State of Israel.

There is a reason that to Islamic fundamentalists the United States is the "Great Satan" and Israel the "Little Satan." America is the principle enemy, and Israel the lesser. Historically, the Jews were a minority people in the Arab world, treated reasonably for the most part, but definitively as inferiors—'*dhimmi*'—plagued with harsh taxes and prejudicial laws. The concept of such a minority actually securing its independence, and not only that, but doing so in the midst of the Arab realm, is anathema. Combined with that is the fact that the Arabs see Israel as an extension of the West. It is a state founded by European Jews, and built in the democratic tradition of the West. It is seen as a modern-day Crusader state, a weapon that Western governments can use to cause further dishonor to the Arab world. Arab leaders routinely refer to Israel as a tool of the imperialists and the West. The fundamentalists do not hate the West because of Israel, they hate Israel as part of their unending hatred of the West.

Question 50:
Why do terrorists feel threatened by American values?

ANSWER: We represent freedom, democracy, success, and personal choice. According to terrorist doctrine, all this must be destroyed.

ANALYSIS: Beyond the notion of *'dar al Islam'* and *'dar al harb'* (see Question 23) and the Muslim fundamentalist desire to create an entire world ruled by Arabs in a unified, Muslim fundamentalist state, terrorists fear the West because of the freedom it represents. We have already seen the strong link between terrorists and tyranny; their methods are the same. Tyrants rule by exerting harsh control over their population, and through fear and intimidation. America and the West represent all that is opposed to that type of regime, including equal rights for women and minorities, freedom of religion, an open, free economy and educational system, and personal choice.

American culture works, and because it works, it influences the societies in which the terrorists live, threatening the traditional aspects on which they, politically or religiously, base their lives. The American attitude of "I'm okay, you're okay"—"Lets agree to disagree"—"Difference and diversity is what makes us strong"—"Free to be you and me"—"You can grow up and be anything you want"—is frightening to people scared of change and is abbhorent to the terrorists.

The terrorist is threatened by diversity. Freedom is not part of the terrorist or fundamentalist lexicon.

Question 51:
What is the American attitude toward Islam?

ANSWER: One of openness, yet total misunderstanding.

ANALYSIS: The West, especially the United States, is open to a wide variety of people, customs, attitudes, and religions. That is what makes America great.

The comfort level Westerners feel about traditions different from their own is higher when there is some common shared ground or principle. The three most practiced religions in the United States—Christianity, Judaism, and Islam—are all monotheistic religions, sharing belief in one God and common descent from the patriarch Abraham.

Until 9/11 the only thing the average American needed to know or cared to know about Muslims was that they were monotheists, and that was good. Some might have known that they followed the teachings of their prophet, Mohammed, and that their "bible" was called the Koran. Americans had next to no knowledge of Islamic culture—the religion, the civilization, the philosophy, or the Arabic language.

Now, for many Americans living through the aftermath of 9/11, Islam has become synonymous with terror. It is true that the 9/11 terrorists, and many other terrorists, are followers of Islam and that there are elements within Islam that encourage Muslim believers to engage in 'holy wars.' But we've also seen that it is fundamentalist Muslims that have re-focused their religion's teachings on war and hatred, and that it is fundamentalist Islam and its proponents that are the enemy, not Islam in general. Historically, Islam was frequently more tolerant and open than Christianity, and a major contributor to world culture.

Question 52:
The 1970s were rife with terror. How is today's terror different?

ANSWER: The differences are dramatic but there are many similarities.

ANALYSIS: In the 1970s, most terror was directed at England by the IRA, at Spain by ETA, and at Israel and Jews worldwide by the PLO. Today, the entire Western world has become a terrorist target and there are hundreds of organizations planning attacks.

In the 1970s most terror—even Muslim terror—was political. The terrorists were Maoists, Marxists and Leninists. They wanted to create a revolution against the West because of what they saw as the endemic injustice within capitalist culture. Terrorism almost everywhere was supported, funded, and directed by the USSR. Today, religious fundamentalism and hatred derived from that fundamentalism are often the most important motivations for terrorists.

The weapons of the 1970s were simpler—today the potential for destruction is far greater. There were no weapons of mass destruction then, or at least not ones on which terrorists could get their hands. While it was always available for those who sought it out, entire bodies of literature and practice manuals for bomb-making are now within easy access for anyone with an Internet connection. As anti-terror systems improve, so too do the terrorists, and their attacks become more deadly and far-reaching.

Question 53:
Why did the United States not anticipate 9/11?

ANSWER: The United States was caught off guard. They misunderstood the extent of the hatred felt towards them.

ANALYSIS: The United States is the most powerful country in the world, with the most powerful and most advanced security apparatus—and yet, on September 11 2001 the terrorists succeeded.

It is important to understand that before 9/11, US intelligence and decision makers were hardly aware of the tremendous hatred that was harbored toward America by a large part of the world. Because of this ignorance, US officials and intelligence personnel were not asking the right questions or monitoring the right people. They weren't reading critical documents in the proper languages. The United States lived in a world of high-tech services and sophisticated, advanced tools of war, and was oblivious to an entire world of terror that lived under the radar of their sophisticated systems.

The United States had a great deal of information, but lacked the perspective with which to understand it. Emphasis was placed on computers and satellite spying, when what was needed was active agents and informants, especially in the Muslim world—and even those they had were barely used. Reuel Gerecht was a CIA officer who worked for nine years on the Middle East. He quotes a retired CIA officer as saying "the CIA probably doesn't have a single truly qualified Arabic-speaking officer of Middle Eastern background who can play a believable Muslim fundamentalist…"

The United States did not allow itself to see the writing on the wall—the hatred by another part of the world for all that they held to be sacred and important.

Question 54:
Why couldn't the United States prevent 9/11?

ANSWER: That is asking too much. They were prepared—but not for the enormity of 9/11.

ANALYSIS: Following the 1993 attack against the World Trade Center, when one thousand people were injured and six murdered by *al Qaeda* terrorists, security was increased in the area, especially in the area of the parking garage where the original attack took place. The Pentagon and the White House are constantly surrounded by high level security. Even if people anticipated that there would be another attack, and even if the authorities imagined that an attack might come from the air, it was unfathomable to think it possible that four hijacked planes would turn into kamikaze weapons. One reason for the terrorists' success was that they launched a low-tech plan against a high-tech system. They hijacked planes with simple tools—box-cutters—that would seldom catch anyone's eye or arouse anyone's attention. Even when the authorities suspected the hijackings, they did not shoot down the planes for fear of killing the passengers. Up until 9/11, hijackers had taken over airplanes and held them hostage in order to have ammunition to make demands, they had never turned the planes themselves into weapons. This was completely unprecedented. Up until 9/11, when planes were hijacked the air force would follow them and force them down. No one—other than a terrorist mind—could have anticipated this scenario.

Some theorists projected that one or two elements might actually happen one day. The closest anyone came to predicting this scenario were those who were fearful that small, private aircraft might hit the towers—accidentally or intentionally—and the towers were built to withstand that kind of impact.

Question 55:
What are other possible attack sites?

ANSWER: An attack can take place anywhere. The more symbolic, public, and famous the site, the more likely it will be a target.

ANALYSIS: Large metropolitan cities, sports arenas, and convention halls are all targets. The Leaning Tower of Pisa, The Eiffel Tower, The Smithsonian, St. Patrick's Cathedral, Macy's—all these sites are symbols. They are famous, public places where large numbers of people gather. They are all targets.

Religious sites, especially synagogues and Jewish schools are targets, as are government buildings, military instillations, court houses, police stations, transportation systems, airports, ships, bridges, tunnels, train and subway stations, and fuel depots.

The terrorists want to disrupt normal life and strike fear into us on a daily basis as we go about our daily lives. The terrorists want to attack the symbols of our lives, of our freedom and of our openness.

Question 56:
How do we better secure our borders?

ANSWER: By being selective and being thorough.

ANALYSIS: Emma Lazarus's poem on the Statue of Liberty hailing America as the country that gives shelter to those who yearn to be free may be noble and worthy, but we need to be certain that those who say they want to be free really mean it, and are not coming to America under false pretenses, hoping in truth to destroy it.

The United States is a great country and has been a haven for oppressed peoples from around the world who come and find sanctuary and freedom, work hard and succeed in rebuilding their lives. That doesn't have to end—but it can only continue if it is done with scrutiny and vigilance.

The West, and especially the United States, cannot allow just anyone to enter their countries. Visa laws and other entrance laws are on the books—they need to be better policed and enforced. Thorough background checks should be a requirement before allowing 'strangers' to enter. Those seeking asylum or entry into the United States should be sponsored by US citizens who are above reproach, and their contacts and addresses should be checked before, during, and after their arrival. Students should be officially enrolled in real schools, and should be attending those schools, and if they are not, they should be deported. This is not a problem of illegal workers or drug smugglers crossing the Mexican border. The problem is far greater and more dangerous and needs to be addressed.

Canada makes it very easy for anyone, including terrorists, to enter their country, especially as refugees. The Canadian–United States border is very porous; it is easy to cross legally, even by car or van, and even easier to smuggle weapons and bombs onto American soil.

Question 57:
How can we improve visa policies to make certain that no terrorists enter legally?

ANSWER: Enforce the existing laws and policies. Hire more personnel, hire investigators.

ANALYSIS: We must stop the terrorist outside our borders and prevent him or her from infiltrating and attacking our homes. The laws for entry visas are relatively strict; they must be taken seriously and they must be enforced.

While the actual application procedure for a visa is fairly stringent, it is easy to fool the authorities because most of the information is not checked against a source. Thorough investigation should be done on all those who want to enter the United States They should be checked against aliases and agency watch lists and the wanted persons list of the country in which they reside, as well as of other countries. In today's Internet era, all this is perfectly possible.

The easiest way to enter the United States is on a student visa, and in fact, some of the 9/11 terrorists did so. Ironically, visa renewals were sent to the aviation school at which two of them had been studying *after* 9/11. Existing laws require a person entering the United States on a student visa to prove they have been accepted at a school, but it is imperative that a branch of the State Department or Homeland Security be set up to ensure the schools are legitimate, and that the students are actually attending and doing what they say they are doing. It is more work for official agencies and uncomfortable for those seeking visas, but, as the saying goes, it is better to be safe than sorry, particularly in the uncertain times in which we now live.

Question 58:
Is airport security effective?

ANSWER: Anything is better than what existed before 9/11.

ANALYSIS: Airport security today is all about impressions. Its purpose is to give the impression that you might be searched and interrogated, and that you have a chance of being intercepted. Sophisticated x-ray machines and well-trained inspectors are just a beginning, and confiscating nail clippers is just a gesture to show that things are being done.

The only truly effective way of conducting security at airports is by profiling. Pulling over every seventh person at random is just not effective—you don't need to search a seventy-year-old carrying an oxygen tank. That's when airport security becomes annoying, not comforting or a necessary distraction.

The best way to improve airport security is to pay workers a decent wage and allow for the possibility of personal growth and promotion. If luggage handlers and maintenance crews were well paid they would not be tempted to take bribes and turn a blind eye to people who ask them to do something irregular or suspect.

High-tech is important in airports, but it must be used well. Searches and more searches, and delays and long lines make travelers jittery. And jitters are exactly what profilers look for in potential terrorists.

Question 59:
Profiling sounds so discriminatory. Is it really one of the ways to stop terrorists?

ANSWER: Yes, it is. Because profiling effectively allows security to focus on potential terrorists and does not clog the system unnecessarily.

ANALYSIS: Terrorist profiling is a simple and effective system. It suggests that there are certain commonalities amongst many terrorists and when a person exhibits some of them they should be questioned. If a person has visited Afghanistan and Somalia recently and also dropped into Germany for a day he is a candidate for a serious interrogation, as those are all countries where terrorists have been known to train, plan attacks, obtain materials, and receive funding.

Profiling works by immediately eliminating people who are least likely to be terrorists, while focusing on those who best fit the alert. Profiling means no more searches and interrogations of harried mothers with four children unless they exhibit strange behavior. Profiling in the United States should start with non-US citizens and anyone who has traveled to countries that support terror without good explanations. Whether the non-American be German, or French, or Saudi Arabian, does not matter. However, there is simply no getting around the fact that most of the terrorism against the United States over the past twenty years has been carried out by Middle-Eastern men between the ages of seventeen and forty. That became abundantly clear after 9/11.

Profiling is a vitally necessary precaution in the fight against terror. Passengers may feel harassed, particularly if they fall into a 'suspicious' category, but if they are innocent they should realize that this is all being done for their safety.

Question 60:
What are the most vulnerable points and the weakest links in the fight against terror?

ANSWER: The sea, ships, gas stations, and gasoline trucks.

ANALYSIS: The oceans and seas are vast—and they are one of the most used tools of trade for terrorists. The sea is important as a way of smuggling and moving materials and people around. Ships the size of ten city blocks are manned by only five to ten people. Anything could be in the hull and anything could be brought on board. If the crew is part of the conspiracy or hired by the terrorists, the weapons or the terrorists need not even be smuggled aboard, they can be in plain sight. The chances of finding something on a ship, or of adequately inspecting cargo and finding illegal or terrorist-related items is slim, because so few interiors and complete cargo holds are inspected. The sea is a major weakness in the anti-terrorist security system.

Gas stations are very easy targets and must be better protected. More care must be taken when choosing their locations. Gas stations should be removed from city centers and densely populated areas as well as from major traffic intersections. As of now, there are clear zoning laws limiting the location of gas stations for safety and environmental reasons—they need to be amended to include security and terror prevention.

The next most dangerous weapon of attack open to terrorists within the United States is the huge flotilla of trucks used to deliver gasoline. If they contain gasoline, they can be ignited along any highway or in front of any building. If the trucks contain other substances, they can be dumped anywhere. Many of the 9/11 terrorists had truck licenses for transporting hazardous materials.

Question 61:
How can the terrorists use the sea to attack?

ANSWER: By using the sea as a launching pad or even as a base for a bomb.

ANALYSIS: The easiest way to attack the United States today would be to put a bomb on a freighter and blow the ship up as it sails into port or sits there docked. Imagine a ship entering New York harbor, Boston, or San Francisco, with a bomb on it. It would be undetectable and it would be devastating.

The same ship could be used to launch drones (unmanned model planes) with spray systems on them. Drones are model planes bigger than large birds and they fly very low. If launched, they are hard to detect unless you are looking for them, because they can be confused with birds taking flight. Drones can literally fly under radar. These drones could drop gas, chemicals, or bacteria on any coastal city. Their spray systems can easily target water systems.

The attacks could be launched from ten miles off coast and still be effective.

Question 62:
How great are the dangers of a terrorist chemical, bacterial, or gas attack?

ANSWER: Terrorists prefer bombs to gas, but they are working on gas, bacterial, and chemical capabilities.

ANALYSIS: Terrorists like bombs more than gas because bombs are easier to make, easier to get the supplies for, and easier to ignite. You just push a button or attach a remote control. Even a simple cell phone will work as a detonator.

Gas, bacterial, and chemical attacks require a system for disseminating the noxious, deadly material, and therefore attacks using them would require sophistication far beyond that of the average volunteer terrorist.

Terrorists are like petty thieves—they look for the easiest method to perpetrate their horrors.

Question 63:
Is a National ID a good idea?

ANSWER: It is a very good idea. A National ID is an excellent way to clamp down on terrorists.

ANALYSIS: Civil libertarians may hate the idea, but a national system of identification is a harmless tool that will make life much harder for terrorists and much easier for law enforcement and attack prevention.

Many democratic countries throughout the world already use national ID cards and it empowers their citizens without taking away their freedoms. It just makes it easier to know who is who. Germany, Belgium, Spain, Finland, Argentina, Japan, Hong Kong, Thailand, and Israel all use national ID systems.

In actuality, the United States already has a pseudo ID system as it is—the driver's license, or, for those people who don't drive, a non-driver's license ID. Without thinking about it, we are constantly asked for and unthinkingly hand over our licenses to prove we are who we say we are. Student IDs and work tags often serve the same purpose, but they are easier to forge and their production is not regimented.

There might be nothing illegal about walking around without an ID, but even today, if the police have reason to approach you, and you don't have an ID, you will probably be taken in for questioning and even spend the night in jail until they can figure out who you really are. We have a system. Now we need a uniform system.

Question 64:
Is it safe for Americans to travel abroad?

ANSWER: Yes, but US citizens should be prudent and careful while doing so. Consult the State Department's travel advisory on its website and use it as a guide.

ANALYSIS: Americans who travel or who live abroad must recognize that they are potential terrorist targets.

When traveling, especially in some parts of the world, it is essential to take certain precautions to maintain your personal safety: be especially careful traveling throughout the Middle East and the Far East, including the Philippines and Pakistan. Keep your guard up in Europe. If you follow a few basic rules, you will be fine:

- Always be aware of your environment and stay alert.
- Vary your routine.
- Do not take waiting taxis—order one or hail one.
- Be suspicious of people who are loitering.
- Be suspicious of people who try to befriend you.
- Always carry emergency numbers with you, including that of the closest US Embassy.
- Carry a photocopy of your passport; the original should be in a safe or other secure place.
- Try to avoid large gatherings of Americans.
- Try not to be too obviously American.
- In a potentially dangerous country, check in with the US Embassy upon your arrival.

Once you realize that you are a potential target it is easier to protect yourself. In actuality it is even easier than protecting yourself inside America.

Question 65:
What has been the role of the United States and the CIA in terrorism?

ANSWER: Unfortunately, the CIA has a checkered past when it comes to terrorism.

ANALYSIS: Sometimes mistakes are made, and the CIA and the United States have made many when it comes to terror. Their worst mistake was in underestimating Osama bin Laden and the *Taliban* in Afghanistan. It was the United States and the CIA that trained bin Laden's men and the *Taliban* forces so that they would fight against the Soviet Union in the 1970s and 1980s.

Conventional wisdom has it that the CIA was short-sighted (rather than downright ignorant) and that they believed that the bigger problem was the Soviets in Afghanistan. Since the United States could not remove the Soviets from Afghanistan themselves, they invested huge amounts of money, training, and weapons to help the *Taliban* remove the Soviet forces. At the time, the *Taliban* were called freedom fighters; there were even Hollywood movies made (including a Rambo movie) that depicted them as great warriors, friends of America, and defenders of democracy. The *Taliban* were bolstered in training and assets, as well as in name and reputation, while in reality they were thugs and terrorists who hated the West and everything it stood for—especially the United States.

The United States and the CIA have a similar history in certain South and Central American countries where they ended up supporting the wrong side.

Question 66:
Why don't intelligence agencies cooperate and share intelligence and information nationally and internationally?

ANSWER: Turf, egos, and personalities get in the way.

ANALYSIS: On the national level, turf wars between the FBI, CIA, NSA, DOD and local and state police departments exist because of the competition for budgets, resources and glory. They also have different responsibilities and are organized for different tasks.

There are also basic problems within the agencies (what we call bureaucratic nightmares) and expecting them to actually be organized enough to share information and intelligence about things they may not have properly evaluated is a tall order. One example of a 'snafu' was the 1993 raid on the Branch Davidians. In February 1993, federal, state, and local authorities surrounded the Texas ranch of cult leader David Koresh on the pretext of a trumped-up drug charge. In a tragic misunderstanding or miscommunication, federal authorities shot banned, internationally prohibited gas into the ranch compound. The roof was ignited and most of the men, women and children inside the compound—all devotees of Koresh—were killed.

On the international level it's the same ego trip, but on a larger scale. Countries fight with one another and compete for the same sources and materials. They only share intelligence when pressured and often what they give is disinformation—deliberately planted in order to mislead the competition, i.e. another country. This is more than a shame, because so much can be learned and gained by sharing.

Question 67:

In the war against terror, how do you know who your friends are?

ANSWER: Simple. Your friends are those who adopt a genuine no tolerance policy towards terrorism.

ANALYSIS: Since 9/11, many countries and world leaders have joined forces with the United States to fight terror wherever it happens and whoever perpetrates it. They have adopted a policy of zero tolerance. Most countries around the world have pledged to help fight terror. Some have done so publicly and others will help behind the scenes. The entire democratic world is united in this, including the former Soviet bloc. The Arab world is also helping—Egypt and Jordan are providing important intelligence and insights.

There are, however, certain countries that try to get around their publicly proclaimed policies of fighting terror by saying one thing and doing another. Not surprisingly, the best examples of regimes that assert that they reject terror and yet, at the same time, support terror are: the Palestinian Authority, Saudi Arabia, Yemen, Syria, Libya, and Sudan. The Palestinians continue to verbally suggest that they are towing the line, while at the same time they send out terrorists and pay for terrorist attacks. Saudi Arabia does the same. They continue to support their state-run fundamentalist Wahhabi schools that support terrorist ideology against the West. They even send financial support to the families of terrorists.

The only terrorist-sponsoring country that does not give off double messages is Iran. Even though they have recently begun to deny their connection to certain terror attacks, for the most part, they are proud of their terror.

Conclusions

- The United States is stronger—militarily, morally, monetarily—than almost all other nations in this world. If the United States does not stand firm for her ideals and principles, who will?
- There is no adequate response for actions committed out of pure passion, rather than reason. Terrorists do not hate Americans and other Westerners because of governmental policy, but because of who we are. Appeasing them will not work; they must be fought and defeated.
- American Intelligence did not understand the enormity of the threat of Islamic fundamentalism, and therefore could not anticipate 9/11. Now we know to anticipate and plan for the most far-fetched of events. Specialists in their fields must learn to think like terrorists in the hope of anticipating their actions.
- The United States has revamped her anti-terrorism program. Vigilance must continue. Knowledge and understanding of the ways, customs, and thinking of other societies and countries must be advanced. Governmental and law enforcement agencies, educators, and counselors must exercise extreme vigilance in picking up on cues from people who might be involved in potential terrorist activities.
- Entering the United States is a privilege. Beefed-up border patrols and controls are essential. Immigration and visa requirements must be tightened up. Monies, personnel, and technology must be made available so that thorough checks can be run before and after people enter the United States.
- Airports must invest in employees as well as technology. Concentrate on what is visible to the eye and what is invisible. When it comes to airport security, preparation and profiling count.

- If you are a traveler, be patient. Once a terrorist manages to get on a plane, it is too late. Even in the world today, where we strive to be politically correct, it is vital to understand that there are certain times when it is right and necessary to push the limits of privacy and personal rights, when and where it will mean saving lives. If you want to fly you'll have to agree to put up with it.
- Waterways must be regulated much as airports are. The numbers of port inspectors and the Coast Guard must be increased, and they should be empowered to board any boat or ship to search and seize. A large perimeter around the United States must be set, and intelligence must be stepped up among merchant fleets, harbors, and sea ways.
- There is little that can be done to protect against gas, chemical, or bacterial attacks. That is one of the reasons why it is so important to go after not only the actual terrorists, but the organizations, individuals, and governments that harbor, sponsor, and sanction terror.
- A national ID system is a vital asset in the fight against terrorism. The public must understand that civil liberties will not be taken away.
- The United States must monitor and be proactive with countries where they have intervened to promote stability.
- On a national level, an entire re-haul of US agencies is essential, complete with computer information sharing capabilities as well as regular meetings and shared updates from the highest levels to the operational level. Agencies must learn to trust one another and that must come from the top down. The same should be done on a larger scale by nations who form a pact to share information and to teach each other and learn from one other, nations that really want to fight—and win—the war against terror.

LIVING WITH THE
THREAT OF TERROR

Question 68:

How do you live with the threat of terror?

ANSWER: Living with the threat of terror becomes second nature, like living with the threat of traffic accidents.

ANALYSIS: Living under the threat of terror enhances our understanding of the value of human life, both personally and collectively. You never know when the next attack is going to take place. The only thing you can do is be vigilant and watchful.

Israel lives with the threat of terror daily, and it does take its toll on society, but every day Israelis get up, begin the day, and go about their lives, despite the threat. Living a normal life, eating out, going to the movies, shopping, is still possible. You do your little bit to help the security situation by accepting the precautions imposed on you with patience and understanding—even gratitude.

Some people become news junkies while others shut off the news, not wanting to hear how many potential incidents were prevented. Some switch between the two, switching off when it becomes too much. When terror does strike, it is impossible to avoid the reality, but everyone finds some way to blow off steam; developing coping mechanisms that help keep stress and anxiety down.

Question 69:
What do I do to prepare in case of a terror attack?

ANSWER: Have available emergency numbers and the phone numbers and addresses of family and friends. Monitor events through TV and radio.

ANALYSIS: The odds of a terror attack touching you personally are minute, even infinitesimal. Should you hear that an attack has occurred, the first and most important thing to do is to reach out and find your loved ones and friends and make certain everyone is okay. This isn't as easy as it sounds, because in certain circumstances, phone lines and cellphone connections go down or the networks are flooded with so many callers that they crash. Some people are just unaware that something has happened and are out of contact. Try and remember where people said they would be. Monitor the news to find out what happened and realistically evaluate the degree of the danger and the threat. In nearly all cases the attack will be localized and will not affect you.

If the attack has occurred somewhere your friends or family could have been and you can't locate them, contact local hospitals and aid stations. Don't panic, be persistent. Emergency numbers will be announced on television and radio. Focus on remembering what that person was wearing that day, and list any birthmarks, tattoos, or identifying marks that could help others identify that person.

If someone is hospitalized, go to them. Take your cellphone and charger with you, as well as small change for pay phones in case you can't use your cellphone in the hospital. Take the list of phone numbers you made; take paper and pencil. Rely on others—friends and professionals—to help you through, and delegate responsibility to others when possible to avoid being overwhelmed.

Question 70:
Should I prepare a sealed room and buy duct tape, bottled water, and canned goods to prepare for the worst-case scenario?

ANSWER: There are certain things you should always have in your home in case of an emergency, regardless of the terror threat.

ANALYSIS: Even though you'll probably never need them to protect yourselves in case of a terrorist attack, there are certain things you should always have in your home. Some provisions are appropriate and important in case of any emergency—a hurricane, a blizzard, a power-outage.

Always keep a flashlight in your home and make sure you have spare batteries and that you can get to it easily. Candles and matches are also helpful. Keep a battery-operated transistor radio, some canned food, powdered milk, and bottled water in a storage area. Make certain that you have enough for the household for at least thirty-six hours.

Duct tape and sealed rooms are really not necessary, and are more help psychologically than physically. Most people need to feel some form of comfort and empowerment, to feel that they are doing something against circumstances and powers beyond control. Being indoors with windows closed and air conditioners off is enough in most circumstances, and none of us can or should walk around in full protective gear for the rest of our lives.

The basic rule of thumb is that if dust can get in, so can gas and chemicals. The real worry is for those people who were close to an attack site and who might have been directly exposed.

Question 71:
Why call a high-level terror alert?

ANSWER: There are three reasons for alerts. All are important.

ANALYSIS: Alerts really do play an important role in the fight against terror. They are not there simply to frighten citizens or prepare them for the worst.

The first reason for calling a high level terror alert is that the authorities have multiple independent sources suggesting that there is an imminent attack.

The second reason is that authorities have partial information—but not enough. So they play a game with the terrorist by saying "we know about you and we are looking for you", without tipping their hand as to how much they really do or do not know. This can act as a deterrent; the terrorist might choose to abort and/or reorganize if he hears there is an alert.

The third reason is to reassure people that something is being done to address the terrorist threat, that the authorities do know what is happening and have an idea of how to deal with the risk and prevent the dangers that are confronting the United States.

Question 72:
What do the different colors of terror alerts mean?

ANSWER: The colors represent an escalating scale of threat.

ANALYSIS: The colors of the terror alert scale correspond to the colors of a rainbow.

They begin with green and end with red. It is a simple code that enables everyone—even kids—to adjust to a very serious and complicated situation.

GREEN	means low
BLUE	means guarded
YELLOW	means elevated
ORANGE	means high
RED	means severe

Question 73:

If an attack is happening what should I do?

ANSWER: It depends on where you are.

ANALYSIS: If you are a safe distance away from the attack, try to relax. Monitor the news and call your loved ones to make certain that they are all okay.

If you are closer to the site of the attack, go inside, get off the street.

Watch the news to determine the nature of the attack and to find out what to do. If it is an unconventional attack pay careful attention; find out which direction the wind is blowing, bearing in mind where you are relative to the attack site.

Listen to the authorities and experts. In the case of an actual attack, they are smarter than you. Do what they tell you to do.

Question 74:
What do I do if a family member is missing?

ANSWER: Keep calling them. Enlist others to help locate the missing person. Call the Red Cross and local hospitals, they will have hotlines up and available almost immediately.

ANALYSIS: I could say, "don't panic," but it probably won't help if someone you care about is missing after an attack. In most cases, they are just out of touch temporarily, but people do get injured and killed in attacks and you have to find out the truth.

Keep calling that person, or calling places where you think that person might be. Try to remember their schedule for that day. After a while, borrow a phone from a neighbor or friend and use that to keep calling—that way your line will be free when the missing person does call in.

Sometimes, especially in an emergency, cellphones just don't work. Networks become over-burdened with calls, especially in the region of the attack, and will be temporarily out of order. Do keep trying; eventually the call will go through.

In the event that you still cannot get through to the person, contact the Red Cross, local hospitals and the police. Give a specific and detailed description of the person you are looking for. Describe clothing, birthmarks, tattoos, and any distinguishing feature. Take a current photo to them.

In the worst case scenario, go down to a specified Red Cross or FEMA rescue center.

Question 75:
What should we tell our children?

ANSWER: Tell them what you need to tell them so that they feel safe.

ANALYSIS: Children have a sixth sense that can sniff out worry, concern, and fear in adults. In the event of a terror attack, it is essential that you provide them with an extra sense of comfort and explain to them that they are safe.

The message you give your children should be adjusted depending on the age of the child and shouldn't necessarily be kept until after an attack, but discussed in generalities beforehand. The essence of your explanations must be to make them feel safe, without resorting to lying outright. Children have heard of terror; they are never as naïve and ignorant as you might think. They know about it from conversations around the house and from overhearing the news in the car. They may have spoken about it in school or their friends might have clued them in to the facts as they see them. They might even be discussing it amongst themselves. They also know about terror from television, movies, cartoons, and comics. That fictionalized, exaggerated terror may be more frightening to them than the real thing.

Children—from toddlers to teens—need to be reassured that their world will continue, even if altered. They need to know that everyone in their world, from their parents to the police, to the principal to the president, is doing what needs to be done in order to keep them safe and to catch the terrorists. Parents unfortunately need to explain that there are bad, evil people who do horrible things, like attacks of terror. But that "you are safe because you are with people who love you and will protect you."

If children should ask about the random nature of terror, explain that they are right, it is random and can strike anywhere, but that they will be safe from the threat because you take precautions and because the likelihood of them or anyone they know being injured or killed is very very small. Acknowledge their fears and never belittle them, but put them in context.

If someone you or your children know and love is injured or killed, seek professional guidance, and comfort them with lots of love. Assure them that just because tragedy happened to that person it does not mean that it will happen to them—or to you.

Talking about terror is similar to talking about drugs and sex. The kids are going to hear about it anyway, so it's best to let them learn about it from you.

Conclusions

- A society must strive to maintain a sense of normalcy despite the threat of terror.
- It is imperative to keep security high and report suspicious people, incidents, and objects. Everyone, willingly or not, intentionally or not, is enlisted in the fight against terror.
- Have up-to-date phone numbers for everyone you love and care about.
- Find your own level of comfort when it comes to preparedness. Go with your gut. When the worst does happen, don't panic, follow directives, and respond.
- The alerts system must be kept in place. It is a deterrent. Don't panic, but don't dismiss it lightly. Memorize the colors that signify the different scales of alert.
- Trust the people who are supposed to know what to do. Learn first aid, be part of a volunteer system that can aid and assist areas and people in need. Get organized now, people in need can't wait. Get a system in place. The same system can help in other emergencies, such as natural disasters.
- "No man is an island," especially in the case of a terrorist attack. If there is an attack, just because you know you're safe don't suppose that those who care about you know it. Call them.
- Think about what you will tell your children before you speak to them about terror. Be prepared for a barrage of questions and difficult answers. Be honest, within boundaries.

More questions?

Do you have more questions about terrorism that you'd like answered?

terror@tobypress.com is an address devoted to your questions about terror. Email me with any questions you have relating to terror, and I will try to answer them. Your question may appear (unattributed) in the next volume of *What You Need to Know About: Terror.*

Major Terrorist
Organizations

The Americas

The South American National Liberation Army (ELN)

ELN, inspired by Ché Guevara and Fidel Castro, was created in 1965. It is a Bolivian and Columbian Marxist revolutionary group. The ELN gained inspiration from Castro's revolution in Cuba. They hoped to do the same in Bolivia and Columbia. Most of this group's leaders are left-wing intellectuals and have received tremendous popular support.

The ELN has attacked US interests in South America. They protested capitalist enterprises that, they felt, exploited the natural resources and the people of South America. They wanted to exert pressure on US companies and US government-sponsored programs to leave South America.

The exact strength of the ELN is unknown. Their most effective tool has been guerilla warfare. They also kidnap foreigners and locals and extort ransom for them.

The ELN leader, Ché Guevara, who died in 1967, was considered a hero during the student protest movements that took place throughout the world during the 1960s and 1970s.

The Revolutionary Armed Forces of Columbia (FARC)

FARC was founded in 1964 as the military wing of the Columbia Communist Party. Since then they have perpetrated kidnappings, assassinations, and bombings.

FARC is by far the largest, the most capable, and the most mature Marxist group in South America. It is lead by Manuel Marulanda, who uses the name Tirofijo.

FARC is organized like an army, with strict responsibilities and discipline.

FARC specializes in bombings, murder, kidnapping, hijacking, guerilla warfare, and even conventional warfare. Their targets are, for the most part, Columbian military and economic symbols. They are also known to be involved in drug trafficking.

In March of 1999 FARC executed three US volunteers who had come to work with native Indians. They were kidnapped and then taken to Venezuela where they were murdered.

The goal of FARC is to transform the system of government in Columbia. They want it to become a Communist state.

The Shining Path

The Shining Path is a Peruvian terrorist group.

The Shining Path, or *Sendero Luminoso* in Peruvian, was the brainchild of a former professor named Abimael Guzman. It was created in the late 1960s.

Although Guzman founded Shining Path in the 1960s, it wasn't until some twenty years later, in the 1980s, that they took up arms, and gained prominence by becoming one of the most violent of all terrorist groups in the world. They are a Communist revolutionary group and they believe in the total capitulation of the West. They hope to destroy Peru's existing institutions and replace them with Communist ones.

The Shining Path has well over thirty thousand members. The tools of their trade are assassination and murder. In 2001, they attempted to blow up the US Embassy in Peru.

Europe

The Basque Fatherland and Liberty Terror Organization (ETA)

In Basque, ETA stands for *Euzkkadi Ta Askatsuna*, which means The Basque Fatherland.

ETA was established in 1959 as an organization bent on creating an independent Marxist state in Basque Spain.

They have been very active and regularly perpetrate kidnappings and assassinations. They target very wealthy families and raise funds for their causes by ransoming the victims.

Their favorite tools of the trade are bombs and guns.

The Red Army Brigades

The Red Army Brigades is an Italian terrorist group advocating a violent Communist overthrow of Europe. It was originally founded in Italy in the 1960s.

Their goal was to create a Communist revolution in order to change Western Europe. They want to separate Italy from her Western alliances.

Over the years, the Red Army Brigades has been an active terrorist organization. They kidnap people, rob banks to fund their activities, and in 1978, they assassinated Italian Prime Minister Aldo Moro.

In 1981, they kidnapped US General James Dozier.

In 1984, they kidnapped and murdered Leamon Hunt, the head of the multinational forces in the Sinai Desert.

In 1984, the Brigades split into two factions, the Communist Combatants and the Union of Communist Combatants.

The Red Army Brigades is a Marxist group.

The Irish Republican Army (IRA)

The IRA has a long history. They organized in 1916 to fight against British rule in Ireland, and throughout the years have risen and fallen in popularity and activity level. The IRA of today was reincarnated in 1960 as a result of a struggle in Ireland for equal rights between the Catholics and the Protestants. Their battlefront is anywhere and everywhere in Great Britain.

IRA members are Catholics. They attack Protestant-based targets. However, this isn't a religious struggle, but a nationalist one. Protestants in Ireland are descendants of the British who colonialized Ireland, and want to retain British rule. Catholics want independence from Britain. The IRA attack British army sites and hangouts, and informers for the British.

They are divided into a political wing and a military wing. The political wing is called *Sinn Fein* and is led by Gerry Adams. They assert that the political wing exercises no control or influence over the military wing.

The Red Army Faction

The Red Army Faction is a Maoist Marxist terrorist group headquartered in Germany.

This terror group attacks targets responsible for modern capitalist and colonialist activities. They specialize in bombs and drive-by shootings and fund their operations through robberies and ransoms collected following kidnappings.

The Red Army Faction was the successor of the Baader

Meinhoff Group. It was established as a result of the student protest movement in the 1960s.

The group is committed to armed revolution:

In 1991 they shot up the US Embassy in Bonn.

In 1993 they blew up a new prison using six hundred pounds of explosives.

Before its fall, East Germany lent significant support to the Red Army Faction, including funding, tactical training, and advice.

The 17ᵗʰ of November Group

This is a Greek revolutionary organization.

Founded in 1975, the Group named themselves after the student protest that took place in Greece on November 17, 1973. The students were protesting against the newly formed Greek government.

Over the years, governments from many different countries came to Greece to investigate the workings of the 17ᵗʰ of November Group. They were met with moderate cooperation. Finally, in 2002, Greek police arrested the leaders of the group. They were fearful of terrorist activities that the group might perpetrate during the Summer Olympics held in Athens.

There is the feeling that the 17ᵗʰ of November Group had links to high level political and police contacts within the government of Greece.

Asia

Abu Sayaf

Abu Sayaf is a fundamentalist Islamic terrorist group that focuses its attention on the Southern Philippines and is headquartered there.

They have kidnapped Westerners and held them captive, and even murdered some of them. They are responsible for the car bombs, kidnappings, and murders of many Western tourists and journalists.

Abu Sayaf has pledged support and allegiance to *al Qaeda* and the two organizations are loosely connected.

The Armenian Secret Army for the Liberation of Armenia, ASALA

The ASALA is a terror group whose goal is to force Turkey to take responsibility for the Armenian Genocide.

The ASALA is a Marxist Leninist group. It was established in the mid-1970s and has approximately four hundred hard-core members. Their methods of terror include assassinating Turkish officials and blowing up official Turkish facilities. They do this to exert pressure on the Turks to accept responsibility for the mass murder of over one million Armenians during World War I.

The ASALA hope that through a program of terror the Turks will acknowledge Armenian history and pay reparations for the murder of one-and-a-half million people.

The Tamil Tigers (LTTE)

The Tamil Tigers are a Sri Lankan terrorist organization. They are also known as the LTTE and the Liberation Tigers of Tamil Eelam.

The Tamil Tigers are by far the most violent and dangerous of all Sri Lankan terror groups. They want a separate and independent state of Eelam. They are an umbrella organization for a set of guerrilla war units who pounce on the Sri Lankan army and who set up suicide attacks. They ambush and kill soldiers and tourists.

They first came on the scene in 1976. The group was created by Velupillai Pirabakaron and today they number more than ten thousand men-at-arms.

In 1983, they ambushed a military convoy and killed thirteen people.

They have become very adroit at the use of suicide bombing:

On November 5, 2001, a suicide bomber killed three soldiers.

On October 30, 2001, an oil tanker was blown up by a suicide bomber on a boat.

On October 29, 2001, a suicide bomber attempted to assassinate the Prime Minister of Sri Lanka as his motorcade drove by.

On January 5, 2000, a woman suicide bomber blew herself up outside the prime minister's office.

The LTTE presents a formidable challenge to Sri Lankan authorities.

Jamaa Islamiyah

Jamaa Islamiyah is an Islamic terrorist group that operates out of South East Asia.

Their principle activities center around Indonesia, Malaysia, The Philippines, and Singapore.

They are *al Qaeda* funded, affiliated, and trained.

Jamaa Islamiyah, together with *al Qaeda*, is responsible for the disco attack that took place in Bali on October 10, 2002, when several simultaneous car bombs murdered two hundred Westerners, most of them tourists from Australia.

Aum Shinrikyo (Japan)

Aum Shinrikyo means "supreme truth" in Japanese. This is a religiously motivated terrorist group.

The group was founded in 1987 by Shoko Asahar. It was officially approved as a religion by the Japanese government in 1989.

Their objective is to take over Japan and then the world.

The group believed that the last years of the millennium would bring about an Armageddon between Japan and the United States. Hoping to bring about that Armageddon, on March 20, 1995 this group released sarin nerve gas in a Tokyo subway.

Another nerve gas attack was planned for Disneyland in April, 1995. With the help of the Japanese police, the attack—which was planned to co-ordinate with a fireworks display—was aborted and the group members were arrested at Los Angeles airport.

Aum Shinrikyo is very dangerous. They have a lot of money—as much as several billion dollars—and they are capable of producing and disseminating sarin and vx gas.

Taliban

The *Taliban* are an Afghani fundamentalist Islamic faction.

The *Taliban* took control of the Afghan capital, Kabul, in 1995 and turned Afghanistan into an Islamic state. They imposed unprecedentedly severe Islamic law and Koranic principles on the entire society.

The *Taliban* have hosted Osama bin Laden and his *al Qaeda* organization since 1995. It is in Afghanistan, with *Taliban* support and under their cover, that *al Qaeda* train and teach their terrorist operatives and dispatch them on their missions.

Since 9/11, the *Taliban* have been a prime target of America. Although their forces have been seriously damaged, they still control many parts of the Afghani countryside. Kabul has been freed and democratized by the Americans.

Middle East

Al Qaeda, also called *Al Qadr*

Al Qaeda means "the base" in Arabic.

This is the mother of all terrorist groups. *Al Qaeda* is responsible for more murderous operations than any other terrorist organization.

They are a loosely knit organization that encompasses many different terrorist groups and operates under many different names: The Group for the Preservation of Holy Sites, The Islamic Army for the Liberation of Holy Shrines, The International Islamic Front for *Jihad* Against Jews and Crusaders.

Al Qaeda was created by Osama bin Laden in the late 1980s to help the Afghanis fight the Soviets.

Their objective is to create a pan-caliphate leadership (rule by one single Muslim leader) throughout the world, to overthrow non-Islamic governments, and to expunge Westerners and Western culture. Their primary targets are Westerners and Western institutions in Muslim societies and the United States.

In February 1988, Osama bin Laden declared in a Muslim directive that "it is the duty of all Muslims to kill US citizens, civilian and military, and all their allies."

In June of 2001, *al Qaeda* merged with Islamic *Jihad* of Egypt.

They have been trying to procure biological, chemical, and nuclear weapons. This is how bin Laden operates:

He funds, arms, and trains terrorists from many organizations.

He organizes his own cadre of devoted and loyal terrorists.

He transmits his ideas and has become a symbol of Muslim defiance against the West.

Al Qaeda is responsible for the 9/11 attacks on the Twin Towers of the World Trade Center, and the Pentagon. They are responsible (together with *Jamaa Islamiyah*) for the bombing of a disco in Bali on October 12, 2002 that killed two hundred people mostly Australians. On April 11, 2002, they bombed a synagogue in Jerba, Tunisia, killing German tourists.

Abu Nidal Group

The Abu Nidal Group split off from the PLO (Palestine Liberation Organization) in 1974. They are one of today's most notorious terrorist organizations.

They named themselves after their founder, Abu Nidal.

Over the years, this group has been responsible for the murder of at least nine hundred people. In contrast to many other terrorist organizations, the Abu Nidal Group does not only work alone. They have been known to contract other terrorists to accomplish their missions and they themselves are often hired out to help others. Their goal is to get the job done successfully, whatever it takes.

Until his recent assassination (in 2002), Abu Nidal made his home in Baghdad, where he was hosted as an official guest of Saddam Hussein. It was from Baghdad that he ran his operation.

The details of Abu Nidal's death are somewhat unclear. It was rumored that Saddam Hussein uncovered a plot by his opposition to have Abu Nidal unseat him and so ordered the hit.

Abu Nidal's body was discovered in his apartment riddled with twenty-seven bullets. The official Iraqi report was that he committed suicide.

Al Fatah

Al Fatah, in Arabic, means "the struggle."

This is the original group that Yasser Arafat (Chairman of the Palestinian Authority) created, when he began organizing the Palestinians in 1957, ten years before Israel acquired control of the West Bank and Gaza.

In 1965 they called themselves *Al Asifa*, meaning "the sword." From 1971–1974 they were known as Black September, named after the September 1970 conflict and massacre in Jordon that ended when King Hussein of Jordan expelled Arafat and his group from the country.

Al Fatah is the main branch of the PLO (Palestine Liberation Organization). They are a well-structured organization with an international membership. *Al Fatah* is the largest group within the PLO and as such it wields tremendous power within the Palestinian world. The *Tanzim*, *Al Aksa* Brigade, and Force 17 are all terrorist groups who pledge allegiance to *Al Fatah* and to Yasser Arafat.

For decades they were responsible for numerous terror attacks against Jews and Israelis and other Western targets.

Since the Oslo Accords were signed on the White House lawn in September of 1993, they have severely restricted their terrorist activity.

Today, *Al Fatah's* role in terror is that of sponsor and facilitator. Many long time members of *Al Fatah* are now assuming political and leadership positions within the Palestinian Authority.

Al Gama'a al Islamiyya

An *al Qaeda* linked terror group that is based in Egypt, *Al Gama'a al Islamiyya* is a classic Muslim fundamentalist terror organization. It will attack any group, or organization, person or government that has links to the West.

It attempted to assassinate Egyptian President Hosni Mubarak in 1995.

It has attacked tourists in Egypt.

In 1997, in the Egyptian port city of Luxor, they successfully gunned down a large group of Western tourists while they were visiting the pyramids. This act of terrorism effectively destroyed Western tourism to Egypt and to this very day Egypt is still suffering from the economic blow.

In northern Iraq, there is a large group of *Gama'a al Islamiyya* members who fought with Osama bin Laden in Afghanistan. Almost all the terrorists in this group received their training and experience with the *Taliban* in bin Laden's camps in Afghanistan.

Algerian terror

In order to cast off the oppressive colonial governance of France, Algeria orchestrated a terrible period of terror against the French in Algeria.

Until the 1960s, Algeria, an Islamic country, was a French colony. In order to pressure the French to leave, the Algerians began a reign of terror against them. They used terror as a tool of intimidation and as a way of influencing public opinion against the French at home in France.

After suffering several horrific terror attacks, the French army retaliated—brutally. The French army won their war against Algeria, but lost the battle of public opinion at home. They ousted their political leadership and it was during this period, as a result of their war with Algeria, that Charles de Gaulle was voted into power.

Algeria was granted independence and elected a democratic government.

In the 1990s, Islamic fundamentalists grew strong in Algeria and started pressuring the public to reject Western democracy and all other non-Muslim values.

Organizations like the Armed Islamic Group, the Islamic Salvation Front, the Movement for an Islamic State, the Army of the Prophet Mohammed, the United Company of *Jihad*, and the Armed Islamic Movement all gained strength and popularity within Algeria.

These groups target anyone they see as an enemy of Islam.

Those enemies include foreign and local journalists, secularists and scholars critical of Islam—just about anyone who disagrees with their narrow understanding of Islam.

Since the early 1990s these groups have murdered well over one hundred people.

Most of the active members have been trained in Afghanistan by *al Qaeda* and pledge allegiance to Osama bin Laden.

The Democratic Front for the Liberation of Palestine (DFLP)

The DFLP is led by Naif Hawatmeh. They split off from the PFLP (Popular Front for the Liberation of Palestine) in 1969. They are a Marxist Leninist group that believes that the only way to achieve their goals is through a violent overthrow of the status quo.

They oppose all negotiations with Israel and do not recognize Israel's existence in any form. They consider anyone who even recognizes Israel to be a traitor. That certainly includes the United States.

The DFLP is a very small, but very committed group. Because it is so small it is very difficult to gather intelligence on them.

Hamas

Hamas means "zeal" and is the acronym for the Islamic Resistance Movement. They are headquartered in Gaza. The military wing is called *Izz a-din al Qassam.*

Hamas was established in 1987, modeling itself after the Muslim Brotherhood of Egypt and the *Islamic Jihad* in Egypt. They are headquartered in Gaza with members and cells throughout the West Bank. They are committed to the total destruction of the State of Israel, and have consistently said that they will never accept a state within the West Bank and Gaza.

Hamas is very, very popular in the Arab world and has thousands if not hundreds of thousands of members, and many, many more supporters in the West Bank and Gaza.

Hamas specializes in suicide bombings and drive-by shootings. They have also sent one or two-man shooting teams into Jewish cities and communities with the intent of killing as many as they can before either escaping or being killed themselves.

Hamas is a well-run organization that has divided its activities into several wings: political, religious, military, terrorist.

They are so well run and so popular that they are successfully challenging the Palestinian Authority and its chairman, Yasser Arafat, for the leadership of the Palestinian "street". They also run a full compliment of nursery schools and soup kitchens within the Palestinian Authority.

Since 1987 the entire organization has been led by Sheik Ahmed Yassin, a sickly cleric who, some feel, has been on his deathbed for many years. Yassin had been imprisoned in an Israeli jail but was traded back to the Palestinian Authority after a botched assassination attempt on the life of Khaled Mashal, a *Hamas* political leader in Jordan.

Hamas is by far the largest Islamic fundamentalist group in the West Bank and Gaza.

Hezbollah *(or Hezbullah)*

Hezbollah, in Arabic, means the "Party of God".

They came into existence after Israel's invasion into Lebanon in 1982 as a Muslim resistance group under the leadership of Sheik Hassan Nasrallah.

Based in Lebanon and bent on the destruction of Israel as well as the West: *Hezbollah* is one of the most active and deadly of all terror groups.

Hezbollah is responsible for the murder of hundreds of Americans.

Hezbollah has successfully operated terrorist attacks and kidnapped many foreigners in Lebanon.

In 1983 alone they killed well over 320 Americans in Lebanon. In April 1983 they set off a car bomb at the US Embassy in Beirut, killing sixty-three people. In October, they drove a truck into the

US Marine barracks in Beirut exploding the building and killing 241 soldiers.

They have regularly kidnapped Western journalists and diplomats including the special envoy of the Archbishop of Canterbury, Terry Waite. They conduct raids across the Israeli border and have sent gliders across the border with terrorists aboard to infiltrate Israel and kill innocent Israelis.

The Islamic Jihad (Egypt)

The *Islamic Jihad* was the original *jihad* organization centered in Egypt. *Islamic Jihad* is the father of all Islamic terrorist groups. They are deeply aligned with *al Qaeda* and, in fact, the two organizations merged in June of 2001.

Jihad's root meaning is to "endeavor" or "strive" or "struggle." Many *jihad* groups and other Islamic terror groups, including the terror group *Hamas*, have modeled themselves after the *Islamic Jihad.*

One of their strengths is that, alongside their terrorist activities, the *Islamic Jihad* sponsors educational facilities, soup kitchens, and a variety of other socially conscious and humanitarian activities. Consequently they are very popular, especially among the young, the poor, and the uneducated in Egypt.

At the same time, they are responsible for the assassination of Egyptian President Anwar Sadat and numerous other attacks in Egypt.

Islamic Jihad is revered by most other Islamic-based terrorist organizations.

Popular Front for the Liberation of Palestine (PFLP)

The PFLP is a Marxist Leninist group which was founded in 1967 by George Habash.

The PFLP is responsible for a long list of terror attacks perpetrated against Israeli and Western targets. They do not recognize Israel's right to exist and oppose all negotiations with Israel.

Syria offers the PFLP refuge and protection.

Their most successful attack was in October 2001, when they assassinated Israel's Minister of Tourism (and a former IDF General), Rehavam Ze'evi, in a Jerusalem hotel.

PFLP (GC)

The PFLP (GC) is a splinter group of the PFLP. The General Command (GC) of the PFLP split off in 1968 when Ahmed Jabril, one of the PFLP heads, became frustrated by the leadership of George Habash.

The PFLP (GC) has perpetrated numerous attacks against Israel using hot air balloons and motorized hang-gliders.

They receive support and assistance from Syria and Iran.

PFLP (SC)

The PFLP (SC) is the Special Command (SC) of the PFLP. This group split off from George Habash's PFLP in 1979. Their leader is Abu Salim.

Their highest profile attack was in 1985 when they attacked a restaurant in Spain that was a hangout for the US military. Eighteen people were murdered in the bomb attack.

The PFLP (SC) receives aid from Syria, Lebanon, and Iraq.

The Kurdish Workers Party (The PKK)

The PKK is a terror group dedicated to liberating Kurdistan from Turkey.

They are a Marxist-Leninist group that targets Turkish politicians and Turkish sites in order to intimidate Turkey and force Turkey to give them their own independent state.

They were founded in the 1970s by a man named Abdulah Ocalan. He has since been arrested and tried by Turkish authorities.

After his trial he appealed—unsuccessfully—to the PKK and other Kurdish freedom fighters to put down their weapons and negotiate for their national liberation.

The PKK's main objective is to disrupt and damage the tourism industry in Turkey. They want to make people afraid to visit, and to hurt Turkey economically.

Over the years, hundreds of people have been killed by the PKK and their terror. In 1993 alone, in the month of July, ninety-four people were murdered in terror attacks by the PKK.

The Palestine Liberation Front (PLF)

The Palestinian Liberation Front is a splinter group of the Popular Front for the Liberation of Palestine.

The PLF broke away from the PFLP in the 1970s.

The PLF's objective is the total destruction of Israel and anyone allied with Israel. The PLF was under the leadership of Abu Abbas until his arrest in April, 2003 in Iraq, by US forces.

This is the group responsible for the hijacking of the Achille Lauro luxury cruise liner. In this notorious terror attack, on October 6, 1985, the terrorists murdered a 69-year-old Jewish man from New York who was confined to a wheel chair, and then threw his body overboard. After two days of terror, drama, and negotiations the terrorists were promised and given their freedom. An Egyptian Air airliner flew them out, but on route to freedom a US F-14 forced the plane down in Sicily. The terrorists were arrested and convicted, but the saga did not end there. On February 26, 1996, one of the terrorists, Youssef Magied al Molqi, disappeared while on a twelve day furlough from prison. An international diplomatic crisis ensued as the United States pressed hard for the Italians to search and re-apprehend him. He was finally found.

The PFL have also sent terrorists into Israel using hang-gliders and small rubber boats.

The Palestine Liberation Organization (PLO)

The PLO is the umbrella organization for the majority of Palestinian groups.

Yasser Arafat founded the group in Egypt in 1963; he remains its leader.

Throughout the 1960s, 1970s, and 1980s the PLO was responsible for horrific acts of terror worldwide, as well as in Israel. In
November 1971, they assassinated the Jordanian prime minister during
a visit to Egypt. Later that year, they attempted an assassination of
the Jordanian ambassador to London. In February 1972, they blew
up a German electric plant and a Dutch gas plant. In May 1972, they
hijacked a Sabena airliner on route from Vienna to Tel Aviv. That
same month, with the help of the Japanese Red Army, they entered
the arrival terminal in Ben Gurion Airport in Tel Aviv, Israel and
sprayed it with machine-gun fire, murdering twenty-four people,
mostly Christian pilgrims.

Following the signing of the Oslo Accords (a pact between
Israel and the Palestinian Authority) on the White House lawn in
1993, the PLO is assumed by most governments to be a group that
has ceased its terrorist activities.

Israel has observed otherwise. The PLO's military branch is
responsible for continued terrorist attacks in Israel against settlers (those
who live in the West Bank and Gaza) and other Israeli targets.

The Islamic Jihad (Palestine)

The Palestinian *Islamic Jihad* is a fundamentalist Islamic terrorist
group operating out of Gaza.

It was established in the 1970s, modeled after the *Islamic Jihad*,
Egypt. They are an extreme religious group with connections to Iran
and Syria, countries that also fund them.

They are headquartered in Syria, but the *Islamic Jihad* has set
up a center of operations in Gaza where they are welcome and very
popular.

The objective of the *Islamic Jihad* is to establish a Muslim state
in the entirety of 'Palestine', which includes all of modern-day Israel.
They reject any non-Muslim presence in any section of Palestine and
will use any and every means to expel the modern day Crusaders, the
"evil Zionists" as they call them.

Anyone who negotiates with Israel is in their eyes a traitor
and cannot be trusted to lead the Palestinian people. They therefore

reject the Palestinian Authority and will not yield to their calls for cease-fires.

Kach and *Kahane Chai, (JDL)*

Kach and *Kahane Chai* are offshoots of the original, American-based, Jewish Defense League (JDL). These groups now operate out of Israel.

The JDL was established by Rabbi Meir Kahane in New York City in the 1960s to defend and protect elderly Jews in difficult New York neighborhoods and to fight for the rights of oppressed Jews around the world—especially for Soviet Jews.

Rabbi Kahane moved to Israel, bringing his ideas and politics with him. In Israel he established an organization called *Kach*, which is best translated in this context as "Take That!" He advocated transfer of the Palestinians out of Israel and the territories as a solution to the Israeli-Palestinian conflict.

Kahane was elected to the Israeli parliament but was stripped of his position after his party was deemed racist, and a propagator of hatred.

Kahane was assassinated outside the New York Hilton Hotel in May 1990, by members of *al Qaeda*.

Kahane Chai, which in Hebrew means "Kahane lives", was established in memory of Meir Kahane by his son Binyamin. Binyamin and his wife were murdered by terrorists in December 2000, as they were dropping their child off at school.

In February of 1994, Dr. Baruch Goldstein, a Kahane supporter, murdered twenty-nine Muslims while they prayed in the Tomb of the Patriarchs in Hebron, a holy site for Jews and Muslims. Because of Goldstein's affiliation with *Kach* and *Kahane Chai*, the Israeli government banned the organizations. The Supreme Court upheld the decision.

Resources

Recommended Reading

A Durable Peace, Benjamin Netanyahu, Warner Books, 1993, 2000
A History of the Arab Peoples, A. Hourani, Warner Books, 1992
A History of Terrorism, Walter Laqueur, Transaction publishers, 2001
A Very Short Introduction to the Koran, Michael Cook, Oxford University Press, 2000
Al Qaeda: The Terror Network That Threatens the World, Jane Corbin, Thunder's Mouth Press/Nation Books, 2002
Fighting Terror: How Democracy can Defeat Domestic and International Terrorists, Benjamin Netanyahu, Noonday Press, 1999
Hatred's Kingdom: How Saudi Arabia Supports Global Terrorism, Dore Gold, Regnery, 2003
Lessons of Terror: A History of Warfare Against Civilians, Why it has Always Failed and Why it will Fail Again, Caleb Carr, Random House, 2002
Origins of Terrorism: Psychologies, Ideologies, Theologies, States of Mind, Walter Reich, Woodrow Wilson Center Press, 1998.
Saddam: King of Terror, Con Coughlin, Ecco, 2002
Semites and Anti-Semites: An Inquiry into Conflict and Prejudice, Bernard Lewis, W.W. Norton & Company, 1986
Terror and Liberalism, Paul Berman, W.W. Norton & Company, 2003
The Age of Sacred Terror: Radical Islam's War against America, Daniel Benjamin and Steven Simon, Random House, 2002
The Arab Mind, Raphael Patai, Hatherleigh Press, 1973

The Arab Predicament: Arab Political Thought and Practice since 1967, Fouad Ajami, Cambridge University Press, 1999

The Arabs in History, Bernard Lewis, Oxford University Press, 1966

The Crisis of Islam: Holy War and Unholy War, Bernard Lewis, Modern Library, 2002

The Failure of Political Islam, Olivier Roy, Harvard University Press, 1996

The Koran, N.J. Dawood (translator), Penguin USA, 2000

The New Terrorism: Fanaticism and the Arms of Mass Destruction, Walter Laqueur, Oxford University Press, 2000

The War Against the Terror Masters, Michael A. Ledeen, St. Martin's Press, 2002

What Went Wrong? Western Impact and Middle Eastern Response, Bernard Lewis, Phoenix, 2002

When Every Moment Counts: What You Need to Know about Bioterrorism from the Senate's only Doctor, Bill First, Rowman & Littlefield, 2002

Women in the Muslim World, L. Beck & N. Keddie, Harvard University Press, 1978

Recommended Web Sites

Centers for Disease Control (CDC)
www.cdc.gov

CDC—For Questions about Immunization
www.cdc.gov/nip

CDC—Fact Sheets
www.bt.cdc.gov

CDC—For General Questions
cdcresponse@ashastd.org

Department of Defense
www.dod.gov

Department of Homeland Security (DHS)
www.dhs.gov

DHS—For Numbers and Web Sites Concerning Homeland Security
www.dhs.gov/homeland/contactmap.html
www.ready.gov

Department of Justice
www.doj.gov

Department of Transportation
www.dot.gov

Environmental Protection Agency (EPA)
www.epa.cov

Federal Bureau of Investigation (FBI)
www.fbi.gov

Federal Emergency Management Agency (FEMA)
www.fema.gov
www.fema.gov/library

For What You Need to Know About Terror
www.fema.gov/areyouready

Immigration and Naturalization Services
www.ins.gov

National Institute of Health (NIH)
www.nih.gov

State Department
www.state.gov

Terror Information in the United States
www.fbi.gov/terrorinfo/terror.htm
www.fbi.gov/mostwant/terrorists/fugitives.htm

The Central Intelligence Agency
www.cia.gov
www.cia.gov/terroris/index.html

The Library of Congress
www.loc.gov
www.loc.gov/rr/international/hispanic/terrorism/terrorism.html

Council on Foreign Relations
www.cfr.org
www.terrorismanswers.com

Disaster Relief
www.disasterrelief.org

Red Cross
www.redcross.org

Terror Files
www.terrorfiles.org

The Institute for Counter-Terrorism
www.ict.org.il

The Middle East Media Research Institute
www.memri.org

The Salvation Army
www.salvationarmy.org

The Terrorism Research Center
www.terrorism.com

Important Phone Numbers

Centers for Disease Control (CDC)
770-488-7100

CDC Immunization Hotline
800-232-2522

Environmental Protection Agency (EPA)
800-424-9346
703-412-9810

Federal Bureau of Investigation (FBI)
202-324-6700

Federal Emergency Management Agency (FEMA)
800-480-2520
202-646-46-2520

National Preparedness Office
202-324-9025

National Institute of Health (NIH)
301-496-4000

Red Cross
202-639-3500

Acknowledgments

Many thanks to my editor, Deborah Meghnagi, for her tireless attention to detail, for sharing my vision, and for enhancing this work with her editorial grace.

About the Author

Micah Halpern

M

icah Halpern is a well known social and political commentator and lecturer. He writes a weekly syndicated column on foreign affairs, the Middle East and terror. He is a frequent guest analyst on TV and radio.

The fonts used in this book are from the Garamond family